**What Every Engineer
Should Know About**

COMPUTER MODELING
AND SIMULATION

WHAT EVERY ENGINEER SHOULD KNOW
A Series

Editor

William H. Middendorf

Department of Electrical and Computer Engineering
University of Cincinnati
Cincinnati, Ohio

Other volumes in preparation

What Every Engineer Should Know About

COMPUTER MODELING AND SIMULATION

DON M. INGELS

Caltex Pacific Indonesia
Sumatra, Indonesia

MARCEL DEKKER, INC.   New York and Basel

Library of Congress Cataloging in Publication Data

Ingels, Don M. [date]
    What every engineer should know ; v. 15
    Includes index.
    1. Engineering--Mathematical models. 2. Digital
computer simulation. I. Title. II. Series
TA342.154   1985   620'.0042   85-13136
ISBN 0-8247-7444-2

MARCEL DEKKER, INC.
270 Madison Avenue, New York, New York   10016

Current printing (last digit):
10 9 8 7 6 5 4 3 2 1

PRINTED IN THE UNITED STATES OF AMERICA

PREFACE

Computers are ubiquitous. They are evolving tools that, some have said, are responsible for sweeping modern societal changes more far-reaching than the industrial revolution. Society is still on the steep part of the learning curve with regard to what computers can do. The rate of obsolescence between generations of computer systems is still only of the order of a few years at most. Consequently, we cannot sit around waiting, but must learn about this new mainspring of industry today. Technical people, especially engineers with their internal drive to make things happen, must feel compelled to educate themselves with regard to such a technological revolutionizing tool.

A brief description of what constitutes computer modeling and simulation is presented with just enough techniques given to get a feel for how some of the simulation software packages involving hundreds of thousands of lines of code were developed.

The iterative nature of the development process is stressed, beginning with the definition of the problem, and carrying on through the development of a mathematical model, followed by translation into a computer program, and ending with validation of the final software product. Rules of thumb and observations from both first-hand involvement in the development of large simulation packages and second-hand involvement as a heavy user of evolving systems are given.

The word simulation has a special connotation to certain segments of the business world, being limited to applications involving stochastic systems. However, it is presented in a more universal sense here. Both deterministic and stochastic systems are discussed. Throughout, a general systems point of view is taken so the material is applicable to all kinds of engineering disciplines.

The mathematical details are limited to elementary calculus and a few details in numerical procedures which are presented as needed.

The book is intended as a springboard for the beginner and as an overview for those desiring a single treatise on what all the fuss is about. Its length precludes an encyclopedic comprehensiveness, but all of the significant aspects of computer modeling and simulation are discussed and put into perspective.

Don M. Ingels

CONTENTS

CONTENTS

ABOUT THE AUTHOR

Don M. Ingels is an Engineering Computer Application Specialist at Caltex Pacific Indonesia, Sumatra. He was previously employed by Texaco Inc., Houston, Texas, and was a faculty member at the University of Petroleum & Minerals, Dhahran, Saudi Arabia and Harvey Mudd College, Claremont, California. Dr. Ingels is the author or coauthor of several book chapters and articles on computer programming and simulation. He is a member of the Society of Petroleum Engineers and the American Institute of Chemical Engineers. Dr. Ingels received the B.S. degree (1959) in petroleum engineering, M.S. degree (1962) in chemical engineering from the University of Oklahoma, Norman, and Ph.D. degree (1970) in chemical engineering from the University of Houston, Texas.

**What Every Engineer
Should Know About**

COMPUTER MODELING
AND SIMULATION

1

INTRODUCTION

A trip of a thousand miles begins with the first step. [Lao Tze]

1.1 PURPOSE

Material is presented which will:

1. Define the concepts of computer modeling and simulation and place them in perspective relative to engineering work

2. Explain the uses and limitations of computer simulation

3. Present methods for developing models and performing simulations

4. Present sufficient examples to be a resource book for initiating computer modeling and simulation.

5. Provide rules of thumb which can aid in the evaluation and selection of computer simulation packages

It is assumed that the reader already knows at least one computer programming language such as BASIC, FORTRAN, PL1, or PASCAL. No instructions specifically for computer programming are presented.

As the title indicates, the book presents material that every engineer should know, and not a complete discussion of everything an engineer should know about modeling. It is not intended to be comprehensive, but rather a starting place, a resource for ideas, and a

1

treatise placing the subject in perspective. A simple but complete example is carried through from problem definition to analysis of the simulation results. It serves as a vehicle for continuity. It also shows the beginner how to use the information in the book to develop his first simple simulation.

1.2 DEFINITIONS

A model, in the sense intended throughout the material that follows, is a system of postulates, data, and inferences presented as a mathematical description of an entity or state of affairs. Modeling, then, is the process of arriving at an appropriate set of postulates, data, and inferences. In the material that follows, the models will be either a set of mathematical equations and logic rules, or a computer program embodying the equations, the logic rules, and the solutions to them.

To simulate is to assume the appearance or characteristics without assuming the identity or reality. Simulation in the present context means exercising the model and obtaining some result.

The contrast between modeling and simulation can be expressed as follows: modeling is the development of equations, constraints, and logic rules, while simulation is the exercising of the model. Developing the model is usually more time consuming, but once done, requires only minimal time for maintenance and further modifications or improvements. The active useful life of a model used for simulations might exceed 10 years if a reasonable amount of maintenance and development work is done along the way.

1.3 MOTIVATION

Of what use are computer simulations? They are extremely useful in answering the questions listed below. By contrasting some of the major uses of computer simulation to alternative methods of solving certain problems, one can begin to get a feel for its usefulness.

What will happen if the operating conditions change?

Amplification: Operating conditions might be physical properties such as temperature, pressure, or amount of material. It might mean changing the type or size of a piece of equipment or even the sequence of processing.

Alternative to Simulation: About the only other way to test the effects of such changes is exploratory testing using the actual equipment involved. This might be prohibitively expensive as in the case of a power-generating system or of a refinery where different

sequences of equipment or different pressures and temperatures are
of interest. In some cases it could be dangerous, as in extrapolating
the conditions for handling explosive mixtures. In some cases it just
might not be practical, as in determining the fuel consumption for
lunar landings or satellite visits to the surface of Mars. The list is
endless, limited only by one's imagination.

What will happen if non-controllable factors change?

Amplification: Examples of non-controllable factors are: the weather,
earth quakes, sun spots, ocean wave phenomena, political climate,
etc. Important aspects of all of these can be simulated for use in solving engineering problems.

    Alternative to Simulation: Trace historical data to find similar
conditions or consult a crystal ball. Of course, this still might not
help in determining the effects of these conditions. If that is the
case, then experimenting with the real system and hoping for the
best might be the only recourse.

*By how much does a critical factor have to change before a critical
response results?*

Amplification: Classical problems in this area are metal fatigue and
resonance effects.

    Alternative to Simulation: Experimental testing is usually the
only alternative. In the case of material testing this can result in the
destruction of the sample. If only one specimen exists, some very
painful and difficult decisions will have to be made.

How sensitive is one factor to changes in another?

Amplification: Multiple runs for sensitivity analysis are a major use
for simulation. For complex systems, complicated interactions of components frequently produce nonintuitive results.

    Alternative to Simulation: Experimental testing might be an al-
ternative in some cases, but frequently it is difficult or impossible to
isolate the changes to only the variable of interest. The result is hid-
den or unexplainable interactions and consequently little or no gains
in understanding sensitivity to changes.

    In addition to providing a much more flexible and frequently less
expensive vehicle for answering the questions highlighted above, simulation has other benefits. It can be used for design studies. Multiple
runs using various configurations can be used to home in on design
parameters. "What if" studies are easily and fruitfully done via simulations. The effects of constraints, whether due to physical properties
(like material failure), safety policies, or political edicts can easily be
determined.

One aspect of simulation always generates controversy and at the same time contributes to better understanding. That is the explicit statement of assumptions. When a phenomenon is under study, many individuals have a mental conception of how it should behave. These mental models have implicit assumptions which the owner frequently cannot verbalize. There is the "gut feeling" about what is correct. Unfortunately, "gut feelings" cannot be conceptualized, cannot be analysed, and cannot be rationally discussed. When two independent or willful individuals have strong but contradictory "gut feelings" about how a system will behave under given conditions, little progress is possible since a nonconstructive argument invariably ensues. When the assumptions are explicitly stated, alternative sets can be applied and the results compared to reality to determine which more nearly reflects the actual system behavior.

Frequently, the greatest benefit in computer modeling comes as a result of increased understanding of the entity under study while developing the model. Because of this, it is always recommended to have personnel intimately involved with the system under study participating fully in model development.

Many of the simulation packages in use today required multiple man-years of development effort. This resource expenditure has been justified several times over by the subsequent increase in accuracy, decrease in time to arrive at an answer, decrease in over design of products, and increase in the scope of options considered.

The benefits from computer simulation can be classified as tangible and intangible. Tangible benefits are easily traced and are apparent with good record keeping. Some of the major tangible benefits are listed below.

1.3.1 Tangible Benefits

Manpower savings over traditional methods

Not feasible any other way

Savings in material; doesn't use up consummables, doesn't make off-spec product

Dollars saved due to faster answers, more consistent results

Quite often, the most significant benefits from computer simulation are intangible. These are difficult to trace and even more difficult to assign a dollar value to. They are nevertheless real and worthwhile. Some of the major intangible benefits are summarized next.

1.3.2 Intangible Benefits

Increased flexibility

Increased accuracy

Increased range of operation

New results not available before

Improved results due to standardization

Increased understanding of the entity modeled

Explicitly stated assumptions and constraints

Of course, all of these benefits, both tangible and intangible, don't come free by just popping out of a hat. Major expenses will be incurred in acquiring or using a computer, the expertise required to develop and maintain the model, and the time required to put it all together into a working system.

1.4 CATEGORIES OF APPROACHES

Systems that are modeled mathematically can be classified in several ways, some of which refer to the mathematical form of the equations. One of these classification schemes is presented below.

1.4.1 Classification of Models

Category	Contrasting category
Deterministic	Stochastic
Continuous variable	Discrete variable
Dynamic	Static
Time varying	Steady state
Linear	Nonlinear
Real time	Batch

The categories in the classification scheme given above are not all mutually exclusive. For example, there could be a dynamic model which is linear or a stochastic model which is represented by continuous variables. But, the terms are useful because of their descriptive nature and common usage. A brief discussion of each contrasting pair will elucidate the use of the terms.

Deterministic vs. Stochastic

Deterministic models are those in which if the independent variables are known, then exact values of the dependent variables can be determined, more or less directly. An example of a deterministic model is Newton's first law, simplified as

$$f = ma \tag{1.1}$$

where f is force, m is mass, and a is acceleration. If any two of the three variables are known, then the other can be calculated exactly.

By contrast, in stochastic models, the relationship between the independent variables and the dependent variables contains some random element. So the best one can do is predict the probability of a particular outcome. If a single die is cast, the outcome is uncertain, but there is the probability of one-sixth that the top face will have five spots showing when it comes to rest.

Continuous vs. Discrete

In the examples above, Newton's law and casting a die, the variables in Newton's law can take any nonnegative value and are continuous. It makes sense to talk about a mass of 0.1 grams or 0.101 grams or 0.1011199 grams. The possible values are uncountable and between any two stated or written values, there is an uncountable number of other values. Such variables are said to be continuous.

The single cast die, however, will produce one result from the following countable set: (1,2,3,4,5,6). It will not stop with the top face having 1.5 dots or any other number except one of those enumerated in the parentheses. The number of possible discrete values does not have to be finite, but there must be a clearly stated algorithm for calculating each succeeding value in the set. The set of positive integers is an example of an infinite discrete set. Clearly, each succeeding number can be calculated by adding one to the previous result.

The property of being discrete is not, however, limited to the result being an integer. Suppose there were four men in a room whose heights in feet were 5.7, 6.1, 5.9, and 5.95. Then a list of all the heights of men greater than six feet in the room would be a single discrete number, namely 6.1, but not an integer.

1.5 PHASES OF DEVELOPMENT

The development of computer models and simulations goes through several distinct phases. These can be roughly summarized as:

1. Getting from the real system to a mathematical representation

2. Finding appropriate techniques for solving the mathematical representation

3. Getting the mathematical model and solution techniques onto the computer

4. Validating the computer implementation

None of the phases can be omitted and each takes a different skill. Many engineers and scientists can develop sets of equations which they think will represent the system under study, but they might not be able to solve the equations. A good working knowledge of theoretical mathematics or applied numerical methods will be required to solve the equations either analytically or numerically. Once the solution techniques are determined, especially if numerical methods are required, it is most often implemented on a computer, requiring the skills of computer programming. Finally, the computer results must be validated by checking calculated results against real system data. The organization and collection of such data might require some statistical background to insure proper analysis and interpretation.

Such diverse skill areas rarely reside in a single individual. Developing models thus necessitates good coordination, project management skills, and communication between various individuals involved.

Chapter 2 presents the overall methodology in some detail. Chapter 3 defines a problem and initiates the analysis process while Chapter 4 discusses modeling, getting the real world into a mathematical framework. Chapter 5 describes some of the more useful methods for solving the mathematical model. Chapter 6 discusses both phase 3, getting the mathematical representation onto the computer, and part of the verification/validation activity. An entire chapter, Chapter 7, is devoted to simulation, i.e., exercising the model.

1.6 THE PLACE FOR COMPUTERS IN MODELING AND SIMULATION

Three of the phases listed above are difficult and one is usually neglected during the development of a computer model. The three difficult phases are: (1) developing a written mathematical model, (3) programming the mathematical model so that it is error free and easy to use, and (4) verifying and validating the computer program. An activity that is usually overlooked is documenting the entire effort adequately. Documentation must include the items listed below:

1. Comprehensive and lucid user instructions with examples of both input and output

2. Comprehensive and lucid detailed model description includ-
    ing the development of relationships

3. Evaluation of the model against the intended objectives

While the computer plays an explicit part in areas 2 and 3 above,
it can play a significant part in area 1 also. A person experienced in
both the subject matter being modeled and computer programming will
automatically couch the mathematics and logic in ways which can be
handled by the computer most conveniently or efficiently. Where the
subject expertise and the programming expertise does not reside in the
same person, this will not necessarily be so. There is usually no unique best way to model a system. Consequently, from n different individuals or teams there will come n different models. Furthermore,
a model, once prepared, is not static but undergoes continual updating,
improvement, and enhancement.

1.7 EXAMPLES

The number of computer models and simulation systems is large and
growing. Large-scale commercially available software packages that
incorporate hundreds of man-years of effort exist in virtually every
engineering discipline. Most of these programs originated as sophisticated simulations which evolved into programs for both simulation
and design. The diversity and power of the approach is indicated
below by a brief description of some of the significant systems already
extant and mature.

In chemical engineering there are several of these large-scale
simulation systems available for performing refinery and chemical
plant design and analysis. Three of the larger systems are: ASPEN
[1], DESIGN [2], and PROCESS [3]. This general category of programs is described by Westerberg [4]. Each of them represents an
integrated software system which can assist in the design or analysis
of a wide variety of unit operations such as heat exchange, distillation, reaction, and pumping, and can do the properties calculations
for a wide range of compounds, from methane to crude oil as well as
inorganic ones. Such simulation systems represent large investments
in time and resources, frequently consisting of one-quarter to one-
half million lines of computer programming code.

In the area of reservoir simulation various programs exist for
dealing with black oil (Boss-Aim [5]), thermal (Therm [6]), or compositional models (Comp II [7]) for natural depletion or enhanced oil
recovery processes. These packages also run in the hundreds of
thousands of lines of computer code.

Civil engineering has simulation systems such as COGO for coordinate geometry, STRUDL for structural design, and ROADS, all

part of the ICES (Integrated Civil Engineering System) developed at Massachusetts Institute of Technology. In the area of hydrology, the special problem of snowmelt-runoff [14] illustrates an area which, though highly specialized, is of interest because of the wide geographical distribution of areas for which it is pertinent.

In electrical engineering, the precursor of most circuit analysis programs on the computer was ECAP [8] (Electric Circuit Analysis Program). COSEP-II [10] is another advanced language in the related area of communication systems. The coming together of miniaturization, powerful computational capacity, high-resolution graphics, and rapid response times is leading to such integrated work stations as TEGAS^{TM}tation [15] which can be used for circuit analysis and simulation while displaying not only schematics of the circuits, but simulated graphical outputs such as waveforms. Such integrated applications will provide tools for the upcoming generations of engineers to exercise great creativity and precise analysis.

Mechanical engineers have a variety of packages available, ranging from crash victim simulation [9] to analyzing general manufacturing processes using MAP/1 [12] and SLAM [11]. The latter is a language to both evaluate and design systems with regard to part routing, distances, conveyor mechanisms, machine set up, number of stations, and station initialization. EASY5 [13] is a dynamics model-building package for systems involving pumps, ducts, and hydraulic components. SPEED II [16] is a manufacturing-oriented language which includes capabilities to model such aspects as robotic cells, flow lines, and job shops including tool constraints, setups, lot sizing, and lot tracking. STRUDL is part of a software system developed for civil engineering, but this structural design language has found many uses by mechanical engineers as well.

The brief listing above is not exhaustive, nor could it be since many new programs in each engineering discipline are being developed, especially for use on personal computers. The scope of the subjects covered is, however, indicated.

All of these systems allow the engineer to solve problems too large to be done by hand. They are set up to solve an entire class of problems so that each new variation doesn't require additional modeling or programming. They also provide consistency in results and standardized formats for output so that different users can easily compare results.

As mentioned earlier in Section 1.3, the benefits of computer modeling and simulation are many and can far outweigh the apparent costs. Not all significant modeling and simulation efforts are of the same large order of effort as those listed in the previous paragraphs. Such comprehensive systems have special requirements both during model development and later during ongoing maintenance.

The material that follows is primarily intended for smaller efforts and will not address all of the specific problems introduced into a modeling system because of large size.

REFERENCES

1. *ASPEN*, Aspen Tech. Cambridge, Massachusetts (1979).
2. *CONCEPT MARK III User Manual*, Computer-Aided Design Centre, Cambridge, England (1973).
3. *PROCESS*, Simulation Sciences Inc., Fullerton, California.
4. Westerberg, A. W., H. P. Hutchinson, and R. L. Motard, Computer-Aided Design Centre, Cambridge, England (1977).
5. *Boss-Aim*, Scientific Software Corp., Denver, Colorado.
6. *THERM*, Intercomp, A Kaneb Co., Houston, Texas.
7. *COMP II Compositional Reservoir Simulator*, Intercomp, A Kaneb Co., Houston, Texas.
8. Lindgren, A. G., "Computer-Aided Circuit Design; A Users Viewpoint," *Simulation*, *16*(5):153 (1971).
9. Robbins, D. H., R. O. Bennet, and V. L. Roberts, "HSRI Two-dimensional Crash Victim Simulator," *Analysis, Verification, and Users Manual*, PB-202537, 1970.
10. Coates, R., et al., "COSEP II: A Developmental Communication System Simulation Language," *Proc. Symp. Simulation Languages for Dynamic Systems*, AICA, London, Sep. 8—10, 1975.
11. Pritsker, A. A. B., and C. D. Pegden, *Introduction to Simulation and SLAM*, Systems Pub., West Lafayette, Indiana, 1979.
12. Pritsker & Associates, *Simulation*, *42*(6):291 (1984).
13. Hammond, R., "EASY 5 Dynamic Analysis System," *Simulation*, *42*(1):37 (1984).
14. Marinec, J., A. Rango, and E. Major, "Snowmelt-Runoff Model Users Manual," *Simulation*, *42*(5):171 (1984).
15. TEGAS^{TM}tation, *Simulation*, *42*(4):186 (1984).
16. SPEED II, *Simulation 42*(2):91 (1984).

2
METHODOLOGY

Toe bone connec'a to the foot bone, foot bone connec'a to the ankle bone, ankle bone connec'a to the shin bone . . .

[Anonymous]

2.1 RATIONALE

Solving any problem using a computer involves the application of a certain organized methodology. It includes formulating the problem properly, analyzing the problem objectives and possible solution procedures, developing some mathematical model of the problem, putting the model (including the mathematical solution techniques) into the computer, verifying the match between the computer program and the mathematical model, and exercising the computer program to make sure it sufficiently represents the real entity being modeled. Each of these phases is significant and is discussed in detail below. The iterative nature of the process is shown schematically in Figure 2.1.

Analysis means different things to different people. Here it means taking a critical look at the facts presented, drawing conclusions, classifying results, and taking appropriate action. Suppose, for example, it were desired to simulate a deep-space communication network for the purpose of answering the following question: Is it possible to have reliable color video transmission from beyond the planet Neptune and receive it on Earth? A simple analysis might be as follows:

11

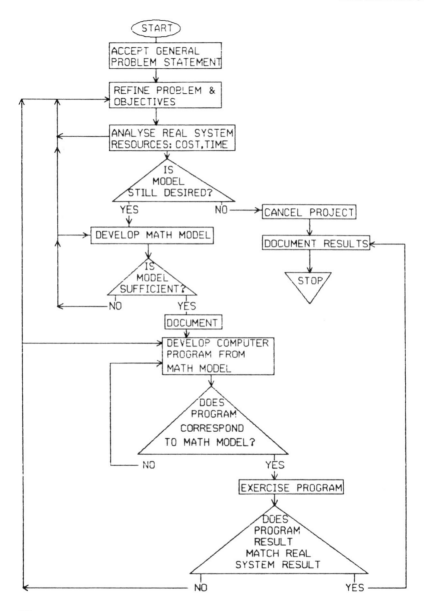

Figure 2.1 Steps in computer modeling and simulation.

Question: Is radio transmission possible?
Preliminary response: Yes.

Question: Can encoding be used to simulate video transmission?
Preliminary response: Yes.

Conclusion: It is theoretically possible.

Now to practicalities.

Question: What weight equipment would be required for space video sensor, transmitter, encoder, and power supply?
Preliminary response: One thousand pounds.

Question: Can the equipment operate under the conditions expected?
Preliminary response: Yes.

Question: How long would it take to get there?
Preliminary response: Eleven years.

Question: Will the equipment be working when it arrives on station?

At this point, the difficult part of determining component relia- bilities and from them estimating what the system reliability or likeli- hood of system operability comes up. These can be estimated using statistical procedures if appropriate experimental data exist. More likely, estimates will have to be made based on some engineering judg- ment. Furthermore, estimates of the costs will have to be made to see if it is all worthwhile. This is the essence of engineering analysis.

2.2 DEFINING THE PROBLEM

The originating statements of most technical problems are rather too general to be a practical guide to evaluating how much effort and how many resources will be required to solve the problem. "We need a program to do distillation calculations" sounds like a fairly definitive problem statement. It has given a hint as to the general area of tech- nology involved, but it has not stated what constraints are staisfac- tory or the precise objectives of having a distillation program. Is it for design or simulation? Is it for binary mixtures or multicomponent mixtures? Is it for well-defined chemical compounds or for petroleum fractions where the exact composition might not be well known? Is it for reacting or nonreacting systems? Should it handle cryogenic con- ditions, or ultra-high pressures? These questions specific to the dis- tillation problem posed are only a sample of some questions that need to be answered before the problem is properly defined.

   The process of getting from the primitive statement of a problem
to something measurable entails talking to the potential users, especially
managers at all levels, since the simulations will be designed to help
them make decisions. They should be asked:

   1. What are the objectives of the simulation?

   2. What questions would you like the simulation to help answer
       today?

   3. What questions do you anticipate it helping to answer in the
       next two or three years?

   The managers should then be asked what criteria they would use
to measure achievement of the objectives and how they will determine
the system effectiveness. Answers to these questions will help the
problem formulators be more specific in what has to be done.
   As a minimum, the general set of questions below must be answered before a computer modeling effort is undertaken.

   1. *Who*   is to use the program?
               will develop the model?
               will program the model?
               will maintain the software?
               can authorize resource expenditure for this effort?

   2. *What*   is the basic objective?
               resources will be required?
               results can be expected?
               range of constraints should it handle?
               are the minimum acceptable performance criteria?
               language should it be programmed in?
               computer should it run on?

   3. *Where* is the work to be done?
               are the resources needed to complete the job?

   4. *When*   is the work to commence?
               is the work to be completed?
               should progress be critically reviewed?

   5. *Why*   is this simulation model necessary?
               isn't it being purchased?
               is it being developed in-house?

In addition to these five basic "W"s, some information about how the
work will be done helps define the problem. After the first tentative
answers to the questions have been collected, they must be analyzed.
The analysis will invariably cause other questions to be raised, and

further refinement of the problem will result. This necessarily iterative process is depicted as an iteration loop between the problem definition block and the analysis block in Figure 2.1.

2.3 ANALYZING

Serious consideration is given to the data collected in trying to refine
the definition of the problem. As mentioned in Section 2.2, defining
the problem and analyzing it are intimately connected in an iterative
procedure. After each attempt to define the problem, the first question to be answered is: Should this project continue? Determining
the answer to that question requires cost/benefit analysis or commit-
ment by the upper management. Even if directed to continue regardless of the costs, the resource utilization should be weighed against
potential benefits.

The specific path the analysis should take depends upon the nature of the problem. But, in general, one must analyze costs, benefits, resources, constraints, technical feasibility, timeliness, assumptions, and connectivity.

One of the major factors which inhibits analysis of systems is
complexity. Complexity can be due to one or both of two primary
causes:

1. Large number of interacting components or features

2. The nature of the components is poorly understood

Not much guidance can be given to alleviate the difficulties caused
by poorly understood phenomena, other than to conduct research. However, if the complexity is due mainly to a large number of interacting
phenomena, some help is available. The chief process in defeating complexity is decomposition. While the concept is simple, the theoretical
thrust in the area of decomposition is active and vital. For example,
the general theory for solving sets of linear equations is well known
and represented by Gauss-Jordan elimination. However, as the number of equations gets large, say 10,000, the general technique, while
straightforward, becomes inefficient, time consuming even on todays
large computers, and costly to use. Most successful approaches to
mitigating the effects of a large number of equations are basically some
form of decomposition [1,2,3,4]. Active research is still going on in
this area.

These successful techniques take advantage of the structure of
the matrix of equations, i.e., sparsity, banding, symmetry, etc.
Sparsity means there are many more zero coefficients than nonzero
ones. Banding means that the nonzero coefficients tend to clump

together in patterns parallel to the diagonal. Even a coefficient matrix full of nonzero elements is handled more efficiently by decomposition into upper and lower triangular matrices than by straight elimination. The details of some of these techniques are given in Chapter 4.

Many of the problems that engineers face routinely can be grouped into logical bundles of processes or operations. Examples are electric circuit analysis, distillation tower design, and structural analysis. Each of these areas is well understood by engineers throughout the profession in the various disciplines. The types of calculations, the order in which they must be done, and the data requirements have been chronicled many times. These same areas, and others, might be classified as mature areas of technology, i.e., they have been around a while, methods for handling them in day-to-day engineering work are readily available, and the methods are not changing rapidly.

All of the three areas mentioned in the previous paragraph have had special computer software developed to handle a wide variety of applications within the given area. Early efforts along these lines include ECAP (Electric Circuit Analysis Program), FRI programs (Fractionation Research Institute), and STRUDL (Structural Design Language).

These software packages were the forerunners of larger more sophisticated programs which grew to include more and more calculations of the specific disciplines. Software systems such as ASPEN, PROCESS, and ICES (mentioned in Chapter 1) cover large areas for the disciplines involved.

These software systems provide a broad spectrum of already programmed (and tested) capabilities. The ones mentioned are available commercially, but many companies have developed their own special software for using internal data and procedures. These software systems should be investigated for applicability before any computer program development is undertaken. Many of the packages have been used for several years with good results as improvements have been frequently made to the systems. Some represent hundreds of man-years of development and improvement effort by professionals in their fields. Thus, development of new programs is not to be undertaken lightly.

During the analysis phase of a proposed computer modeling or simulation project, the availability of existing software should be investigated. If packages exist which will do, say, 80% of what is proposed, the vendor of the package might be approached with a proposal to license or sell his package with the rights of modification, or to generate an expanded system which will perform the desired simulations.

The options then, in general order of preference, are:

1. Use existing available software (in-house or commercial)

2. Hire a qualified software house to modify existing software

3.   Hire a qualified software house to develop new software

4.   Develop new software in-house

Letting a software house develop a new system is ranked before in-house development for two reasons: first, the developers are professionals familiar with both the technical area and the computer, and, second, they frequently can gear up to get the job done significantly faster. Some circumstances such as developing in-house skills or expertise, long-term commitments to maintaining the software, and proprietary information override other considerations and lead logically to in-house development. All of the above, plus costs, must be taken into account when deciding on which option to pursue.

2.4 MODELING

Most engineers deal with models regularly and have a large stockpile available at their fingertips. For electrical engineers these include the common circuit element models, Kirchhoff's node and loop laws, and many more. For answers to relatively simple problems in circuit analysis, these simple models usually suffice. However, if questions arise for which the simple models are insufficient, something more must be done.
The modeling of the solar system, of which our planet is part, evolved from Copernicus' earth-centric model, to Keppler's sun-centric model with circular orbits, to Galileo's elliptical orbits with a few planets, to modern day models. This progression from simple to more complex representations evolved in response to in-depth examination. Unexplained variations between observed and calculated planetary orbits raised questions about each of the successive early solar system models. When a current model cannot explain certain known or observed phenomena in the real system, then the model must be improved.
The progression in model sophistication is invariably from simple to more complex. This is also a sound developmental philosophy for model developers. Model the salient features as simply as possible. Increase complexity in the model in stages to alleviate specific shortcomings. Always work from simple to complex rather than starting off with the most complex model conceivable.
The precept above can show up in the resulting mathematics. Linear models are easier to solve than nonlinear ones, ordinary differential equations are more easily solved than partial differential equations, etc. Closed analytical functions are easier to program than infinite series, Bessel's functions, and the like. Deterministic models are generally easier to deal with than probabilistic ones.
Frequently, a fairly complex system can be modeled by developing a composite of many simple models. Examples of this principle

occur in circuit analysis and in modeling mechanical devices with mass-spring-damper combinations. The general process is closely related to decomposition but is its inverse, i.e., synthesis.

The general methodology for modeling consists of four steps, the last of which is more difficult than the others.

1. Define the system

2. Determine the inputs to the system

3. Determine the outputs from the system

4. Determine the relationships between inputs, outputs, and system internals

2.4.1 Defining a System

A system is a portion of the universe set aside for study as mentioned in the sections above. It performs some task and in general receives inputs to which it responds and produces outputs. In more complex systems, the behavior of any part of the system ultimately has some effect on every other part. However, not all of these effects are significant. Complexity is caused by the sheer number of entities involved or by the complicated manner in which components of a system interact.

The more specifically a system is defined, the more likely a successful model can be developed for it. Part of the definition of a system must include the purpose of the system: what objectives it is helping to achieve and what goals it is directed toward. Sometimes it is very helpful, in areas where there can be various interpretations, to describe what is not part of the system.

2.4.2 Determining System Inputs

Once the boundaries of the system have been clearly delineated, it is necessary to identify all possible inputs into the system. Some of the inputs might be controllable and desirable while others can be uncontrollable and undesirable.

An example of an uncontrollable input is the weather. If the system were an airplane, certainly the weather, temperature, humidity, precipitation, wind velocity, etc., would be of concern. The wind might be either desirable or undesirable depending upon whether it were a tailwind or a headwind.

Major influences originating from external uncontrollable factors can create serious modeling difficulties, especially if, in addition to being uncontrollable, they are unpredictable. Significant external factors cannot be ignored simply because they are uncontrollable or unpredictable. They must be identified and accounted for.

If system behavior cannot be explained by variables and relationships already identified, the possibility of an unrecognized external influence should be investigating.

2.4.3 Determining System Outputs

Since systems are organized entities, designed to perform some desired task, it is usually easy to identify the system outputs. It might not be as easy to identify byproducts or undesired outputs. For instance, when early microwave ovens came out, they functioned as advertised, cooking in a short time, not heating up the kitchen, etc., but it was soon discovered that they also emitted electronic signals which had nonbeneficial effects. For one, they tended to interfere with pacemakers and other small electrically driven devices. This undesirable output could not be ignored. Engineering effort was required for redesigning the system to reduce the undesired emissions.

For both inputs and outputs, the first task is to identify them; to be able to recognize them. The second task is to measure them and, through iterative analysis and modeling, to determine which are significant and, finally, how they are related.

2.4.4 Determining Relationships

The essence of good modeling is to discover the significant variables and develop relationships which describe how they interact. This is at once the most difficult and most rewarding step in the modeling. It is covered in some detail in Chapter 4.

The techniques vary widely, especially between deterministic and nondeterministic systems. The philosophical thrust of looking for cause and effect which motivates deterministic system modeling gives way to averages, trends, and measures of goodness-of-fit of hypotheses in the stochastic system. This difference of approach is important to recognize, first, because the nature of these approaches to systems are so different, and, second, because the expertise for dealing with both kinds of systems seldom resides with one individual. The latter implies a team involvement with its consequent group dynamics which adds to the complexity of a project.

Complexity, as mentioned in Section 2.4.1, is one aspect of a system which decreases the tractability of modeling. The only formal tool for dealing with complexity is decomposition. For those systems in which complexity is due to the large number of entities involved, decomposition can be quite effective. For example, when the number of relationships in a linear programming problem exceeds the capacity of the computer or the software, it can be decomposed into workable-sized problems. The methods for this kind of decomposition are known and reported in the literature on linear programming.

Complexity due to the complicated nature of the system might be dealt with through decomposition if: (1) the overall system is composed of interacting subsystems, and (2) the interactions can be used to relate the subsystems. It is entirely possible that the decomposition will not provide any economy of effort and is therefore not appropriate. The most succinct statement of methodology possible is: start simple, and add complexity incrementally and only as needed. This general concept will be reiterated throughout the book.

2.5 DEVELOPING THE COMPUTER PROGRAM

There are entire libraries devoted to the theory and application of computer programming. The remarks that follow here and in Chapter 6 are intended as an overview and philosophical guide for engineers who already know how to write programs in some higher-level language such as FORTRAN, PASCAL, APL, or BASIC.

There are basically three levels of programming software:

1. Assembler language, which has a one-to-one correspondence to the actual machine hardware instructions

2. General-purpose higher-level languages, such as FORTRAN, PASCAL, and BASIC, which allow one to solve a wide variety of problems if an appropriate algorithm can be developed

3. Problem-oriented languages, such as COGO, STRUDL, and RAMIS, which allow the user to attack a specific set of problems, such as coordinate geometry (COGO), structural design (STRUDL), or information storage and retrieval (RAMIS), using terms more or less similar to those used in solving problems in the particular application area without computers

Assembler language is the most versatile and powerful, in the sense of control of exactly what is happening, but the versatility is paid for by spending more time in details and in developing more lines of computer code to perform a specific task. For example, to add three numbers, find the average, and print out the resulting sum and average might take 14 lines of instructions in assembler language, involving specific registers and buffers in the computer, while a four-step FORTRAN or BASIC program can accomplish the same thing. As the complexity of the problem formulation increases, the simplification advantage of the higher-level languages increases almost geometrically. Where the assembler language has an advantage is in the manipulation of bits and characters and possibly in efficiency of operation. That is, a well-written assembler langauge program will usually perform faster and in less space than a program written in a higher-level

language. However, from the standpoint of efficient use of manpower
for writing ad-hoc programs or making revisions in the code, higher-
level languages enjoy a great advantage.

The net result is a trade off: efficiency of computer operation vs.
efficiency of manpower utilization. With the continuing trend to smaller,
faster, cheaper computers, the efficient use of manpower will usually
win out. For most simulation and modeling efforts it will almost always
be better to program in a higher-level language.

One of the latest buzz words relative to computer systems is
"user friendly." It's not a new concept, but it has received ever-
growing attention, and justifiably so. It means that one should not
have to be a computer specialist or even a computer programmer to
use a computer. Developing user-friendly systems thus opens up the
use of computers to a vast segment of the population that was hitherto
unable or unwilling to use computers. The user friendliness is accomplished by employing interactive video displays which present menus
or options which require only a selection by entering one number,
letter, or word. Writing user-friendly software definitely takes more
planning and effort, but it makes the computer resources usable to an
audience at least four or five times as large as it would be if computer
programming were a requisite for the use of a computer. It is a tool
for increasing productivity of an organization and is thus highly desirable.

2.6 VERIFYING THE MATCH BETWEEN MODEL AND
COMPUTER PROGRAM

As with any kind of modeling, there must be a check to see if the model
represents the characteristics of the real system sufficiently well to
warrant its use. In computer modeling, there is a step between the
development of the model and comparing the model results to those of
the real system, and that is verifying that the computer program
faithfully represents the mathematical model. Verifying this match is
sometimes confused with the final validation process, but it is a distinct phase of work and should be checked separately. For example,
suppose part of the mathematical model is a set of nonlinear algebraic
equations which are to be solved using the Newton-Raphson method.
The verification of the match between the mathematical model and the
computer program would involve two major parts: first, a check to
see if the simultaneous equations have been programmed correctly by
using some values of the independent variables for which answers can
be readily calculated and second, a thorough check of the solution procedure, in this case the Newton-Raphson method, to verify that it
works for various sets of values of the variables. If it does, then
there is a reasonable expectation that it will work for the problem at

hand. Values such as zero or one, or a large positive or negative number, frequently can be used for verifying that the equations have been programmed correctly.

More details on this approach are presented in Sections 6.4 and 6.7. Here it is sufficient to reiterate the principle of synthesizing the system from modular pieces of software which can be developed individually and exercised more or less by themselves through the use of a simple driver routine.

The four sequential general phases of developing computer programs are:

1. Program doesn't compile

2. Program compiles but doesn't run

3. Program compiles and runs but gives wrong answers

4. Program works okay for test case(s)

Usually there is another phase in which the program works for test cases, but not for some special cases. The process in getting from phase 1 to phase 4 is iterative in nature and is called debugging. When a program doesn't work as expected it is said to have a "bug" in it. Hence removing these bugs is debugging.

Only a few rules for debugging are generally applicable, the greatest part of learning how to debug coming from experience. The general rules are:

1. Keep complete documentation of everything done

2. Double check units of measurement

3. Double check values of input data

4. Check individual subroutines before combining them

5. Use trace routines where possible to pinpoint sections of code giving erroneous results

6. Where trace routines don't exist, build in software switches to turn on or off the printing of intermediate results

7. Assume that the error is in the software 99% of the time and in the hardware the rest of the time

8. Check the algorithm logic

Finding bugs during phase 2 above (compiles but doesn't run) is particularly frustrating. The only clues usually available are cryptic messages from the operating system which might not mean anything to an engineer. Don't be embarassed to ask a computer system professional

to decipher these messages. Most will be glad to parade out their
skills to impress an engineer. Once phase 3 is reached (runs but
wrong answers) the burden is pretty much on the back of whoever
wrote the programs and whoever prepared the mathematical model.
Tracing programs can be a valuable asset to use during this phase
if such tracing software exists for the operating system being used.

2.7 VALIDATING THE MODEL

After the match between the computer program results and the mathematical model has been verified, there remains the task of validating
the results. Even though the program is perfect with respect to the
math model, if the mathematical model is deficient in some way, the
computer results will not match those from the real system sufficiently
well to be of any value.

Validation is the step-daughter of the entire process. It is often
neglected and sometimes abused. The trite but true computer axiom
"garbage in . . . garbage out" applies here too. In this case, part
of the input is the mathematical model. If it is no good, all other efforts to massage the computer program are in vain.

Here again, a systematic approach is recommended. For complex
systems for which the entire range of all variables is too large to check
exhaustively, some type of design of experiments technique can be
fruitfully applied. Sometimes, a classical or prototype problem can be
solved using the software to compare the computed results against
known or at least published answers.

This summary has been necessarily succinct in order to present
an overview of an entire approach to computer modeling and simulation.
Details and illustrative examples of each major phase are presented in
following chapters.

REFERENCES

1. Barkley, R. W., and R. L. Motard, "Decomposition of Nets,"
   Chem. Engr. J., *3*(3):265 (1972).
2. George, A., and J. W. H. Liu, "Algorithms for Matrix Parti-
   tioning and the Numerical Solution of Finite Element Systems,"
   SIAM J. Num. Anal., *15*:297 (1978).
3. Westerberg, A. W., in *Decomposition of Large Scale Problems*,
   D. M. Himmelblau (Ed.), p. 379, North Holland Publishing Co.,
   Amsterdam, 1973.
4. Steward, D. V., "On An Approach to Techniques for the Analysis of the Structure of Large Systems of Equations," *SIAM Rev.*,
   4(4):321–342 (1962).

3

DEFINING AND ANALYZING
THE PROBLEM

*Humans are unique in respect to all other creatures in that they
also have minds that can discover constantly varying interrela-
tionships existing only between a number of special case experi-
ences as individually apprehended by their brains, which covary-
ing interrelationship rates can only be expressed mathematically.*

[R. Buckminster Fuller]

3.1 PRIMITIVE PROBLEM STATEMENT

Defining the problem and analyzing the problem are intimately linked
activities. The first vague statement of the problem, or primitive
statement, raises questions which lead to information gathering and
analysis of the information. Further questions regarding the scope
of the problem, refinement, information gathering, and analysis proceed in the inevitable iterative fashion associated with most engineering projects.

In this chapter and those that follow, a specific problem will be
used to illustrate the principles under discussion. Text related to
the problem will be delineated by indenting.

Water Main Problem

Suppose the following question is issued by your boss. "Can we
get water from our current fire hydrants to the top of a five-story
building?"

24

Your first reply is, "But we don't have any buildings that tall."

His query certainly presents some problems. Not to mention the nonexistent five-story building, it is not clear why he wants to get water up that high, where in your plant he might want to get water up that high, nor what quantity of water it is desired to deliver.

3.2 REFINING THE PROBLEM DEFINITION

Once the primitive problem statement has been made, the next task is to gather some information and refine the primitive statement into an engineering problem. This requires some statement of objectives which can presumably be achieved via technological analysis and design.

Suppose the boss is interrogated (peacefully) using the questions from Section 2.2 resulting in the following dialogue.

"Why do we want to deliver water to the top of a nonexistent five-story building?"

Putting his arm around your shoulder the boss replies, "Joe, you're the first to know. We are planning a major expansion. Safety considerations will require us to assure ourselves we have enough water pressure to fight a fire on top of the new building. We don't know exactly where the building is to be sited, we might look at several possibilities, but we know we will tie into the existing water system at any rate."

Following the suggestions in Section 2.2, the major objectives seem to be:

Ob. 1. Determine pressure and volume requirements to fight a fire on top of a five-story building.

Ob. 2. Determine water delivery capabilities of the current system.

Ob. 3. Determine effects of tying into current system at a point to be determined later.

"Boss, since there will probably be lots of possible configurations investigated, I think I'll develop a computer model to help speed up answering "what if"-type questions. While I'm at it, what other near-term questions might you be interested in answering?"

"First, where is the lowest pressure in the current system? Second, if we are delivering x gallons of water to the new building, can we still fight a fire in the vicinity of the low pressure point? Third, what happens if one of the pumps goes down?"

"How about the longer range? Is it confidential?"

"No, I would be curious to know the effects of various additions and modifications to the plant equipment. Also, what is the effect of aging and scale buildup as time goes on?"

"Boss, what criteria will be used to determine if the stated objectives have been met?"

"I think three criteria will suffice:

> *Cr. 1.* The model simulates the steady-state behavior of the current system as shown by good agreement between simulated results and collected operating data.
>
> *Cr. 2.* "What if" studies involving additions and changes in equipment and operating conditions can be made with a reasonable expenditure of resources. This means the program should not have to be rewritten to accommodate reasonable changes.
>
> *Cr. 3.* The model will ultimately be able to include the effects of elevation changes, valves, etc."

"Are there any significant constraints?"

"Yes, any additions or changes will no more than double the number of elements in the current system."

The hypothetical dialogue above might represent a reasonable first refinement of the problem statement. Some idea of why a simulation is desired and how it might be used has been garnered from the objectives and associated descriptions. The problem definition, as refined, leads naturally to a phase of intense information gathering and analysis.

3.3 ANALYZING THE PROBLEM

There are many approaches to engineering analysis, but one that has proven fruitful involves what are referred to as top-down analysis and bottom-up analysis. The top-down analysis starts from the major objectives and decomposes these into subobjectives which are plausibly doable and which if attained will result in achieving the major objectives. The process involved in top-down analysis can be summarized as:

1.   State the problem

2.   State the major objectives

3. Iteratively refine
    a. The problem definition
    b. The objectives (by developing subobjectives)
    c. Methods and approaches to attain objectives

Top-down analysis gives structure to the problem and guidance on how to achieve the stated objectives.

Bottom-up analysis hinges on the end users point of view and the practical aspects of getting things done. The many seemingly unrelated tasks associated with the problem area are addressed, some in great detail, and some just cursorily. These items are described and written down. An attempt is then made to make the levels of detail compatible and to integrate all of the items in such a way as to achieve the stated objectives. The process involved in bottom-up analysis can be summarized as:

1. Have all final users independently state the actions to be taken to make improvements relative to the problem at hand. Specific details are to be included.

2. Eliminate duplicate approaches and activities and consolidate similar ones.

3. Integrate diverse activities and fill in gaps required to meet major objectives.

The top-down and bottom-up approaches are then integrated and iterated to produce a final solution approach which meets the objectives, is feasibly attainable, and is perceived by the users as leading to improvements. Successful applications of this approach have been made in many different endeavors, from corporate planning to writing computer software packages.

A brief outline of the top-down approach applied to the hydraulic network problem follows.

The problem statement and major objectives are given in Section 3.2. These can be broken down into subobjectives along with methods and approaches.

Subobj.	Description	Method
From Ob. 1.		
1.1	Determine height per story	Approximate from existing buildings
1.2	Determine total height	

Subobj.	Description	Method
1.3	Determine pressure requirements	Pressure gradient
From Ob. 2.		
2.1	Model flow thru current network	Simultaneous equations, loop and node
2.2	Validate model	Calculated data vs. collected
2.3	Determine flow in each pipe	Exercise model
From Ob. 3.		
3.1	Assume new outflows at various locations	Simulate using model
3.2	Assume additional loops	
3.3	Write program to allow general network configuration	Accept configuration data as input

A verbal sketch of the first iteration of the bottom-up process is given next. The system of concern is the plant water distribution mains shown schematically in Figure 3.1. System inputs consist of flows into the network of nodes 1 and 7, designated EF1 and EF7, and flows out of the network at nodes 3, 4, 6, and

Table 3.1 Pipe Data

Pipe #	Length	Diameter	Roughness
1	102	8	.000015
2	210	8	.000015
3	97	8	.000015
4	213	6	.000015
5	15	8	.000015
6	150	8	.000015
7	135	6	.000015
8	15	8	.000015
9	85	8	.000015
10	120	6	.000015
11	141	8	.000015

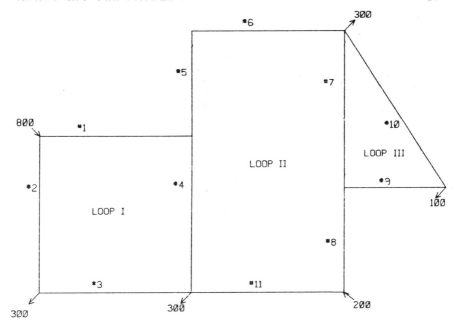

Figure 3.1 Hydraulic network.

9, all in thousands of pounds per hour. The incoming flows might originate from a pump, water tower, city supply, etc., while the outflows would represent aggregate demands for various smaller branches not shown in the network diagram. Each external flow might, in reality, fluctuate and, thus, have associated with it both an average flow and a peak flow-rate that would be of interest to the system operators and designers.

Table 3.2 External Flows

Junction by pipe	External flow
1-2	+800
2-3	-300
3-4-11	-300
6-7-10	-300
9-10	-100
8-11	+200
1-4-5	0
5-6	0
7-8-9	0

The pipe data are summarized in Table 3.1.

The network external flows are summarized in Table 3.2.

The network problem discussion above represents a problem statement and preliminary analysis. Further iterations in the analysis are intimately tied up with the modeling and solution procedures discussed in the following chapters.

4

GENERATING MATHEMATICAL MODELS

The attitude of the engineer to mathematics must be different from that of the pure mathematician. The engineer is concerned with truth, not mere consistency.

[Biot]

4.1 INTRODUCTION

Delineating clearly what exactly is to be studied must preceed any modeling. The part of the universe set aside for modeling is referred to as the system. A system can be defined as follows:

System: a device or process which accepts one or more inputs and from them generates one or more outputs.

$$\text{Inputs} \;\substack{\to \\ \to \\ \to} \;\boxed{\text{System}}\; \substack{\to \\ \to}\; \text{Output(s)}$$

Another way to define a system is as a portion of the universe around which an imaginary boundary is drawn for the purpose of studying what is enclosed inside of the boundary. The imaginary boundary is selected so that the system is a regularly interacting or interdependent group of items forming a unified whole.

Modeling consists of developing relationships which describe how the system behaves. The statements can be either verbal or mathematical, but to be of use for computer implementation only mathematical

models will be of concern here. These statements provide a description of both natural and man-made phenomena. They can be used to
show that the modeler understands the phenomena by being able to
simulate the behavior of the system. Such simulation requires that
quantitative results be obtained.

What is a model? It can be a purely intellectualized image. Everyone carries around in his head ideas and impressions of how things
work. These intellectualized entities are, in fact, models of processes.
Each type of model, be it a scale model, analog model, or mathematical
model, has its place depending on the intended purpose. Critical to
the selection of a suitable model is the nature of the information desired
as well as the nature of the information given or assumed.

Mathematical modeling offers a number of advantages over other
kinds of modeling for implementation on a computer. It enables one to
define variables more exactly, state assumptions explicitly, and to obtain, from complex relationships among several variables, conclusions
that cannot be derived by verbal or other means of analysis. Furthermore, it is often essential to model systems mathematically in order to
verify the model empirically. Through it one achieves economy of effort, efficiency, and rigor while being concise and precise.

Mathematical models explicitly state assumptions. From them one
can derive relationships that inhere in the body of the assumptions,
and derive conclusions based upon the relationships. They can be
applied deductively.

To ascertain the usefulness of the model, one must determine
whether the assumed functional relationships correspond to reality.
The more realistic the model, the more accurate will be the results.
There is, however, a point of diminishing returns in incorporating
details. The real world is extremely complex and if one attempts to
include too many features of reality in a model the result is a morass
of equations containing functions which cannot be solved. If, on the
other hand, the model is too simplistic, it is soon found to give un-
satisfactory results. Knowing that no model can yield a complete description of reality, one must strive to follow a path between over-
simplification and overcomplication which will lead to greater understanding and thus greater insight and utility.

The crux of all model development is to end up with a representation which is as simple as possible but which retains the basic features
and phenomena which characterize the system being modeled. The
overriding principle for developing models is to start simple and evolve
to more complex forms.

4.2 SETTING UP THE MODEL

There are a few general principles which can be helpful in developing
a model. They are summarized below and amplified in what follows.

1. Start with what is known

2. Start simple—work up to complex

3. Iterate

4. Develop large models modularly

5. Model only necessary characteristics

6. Make assumptions or hypotheses

7. State constraints

8. Alternate between the top-down and bottom-up approaches

Each of these principles will be discussed in turn.

4.2.1 Start with What Is Known

It should not be necessary to rederive basic relationships every time a model is developed. The fundamental laws of physics are useful, but it is not always desirable to start from the most elementary building blocks. Known performance relationships should be used if they are appropriate. Such performance equations are often restricted to certain conditions. Outside of these constraints, the relations are not suitable. An awareness of what conditions are applicable is essential to successful modeling. For example, early theory and models of transistors led to the design of successful solid-state devices. However, as the reduction in physical size required by the devices ensued, progressively more serious errors in the models lead to significant disparities between actual and predicted performance. Since the classical theory did not adequately predict the effect of size on performance, new models had to be developed [10].

For the network example, the known data about the network are summarized in Figure 3.1, and Tables 3.1 and 3.2. In addition, the equations relating pressure drop, flow rate, and system properties are known.

The pressure drop due to friction in each line can be calculated from

$$\Delta P = \frac{fLv^2\rho}{2g_cD} \qquad (4.1)$$

where

ΔP = pressure drop due to friction

f = Moody friction factor

L = length of pipe

v = average velocity of fluid

ρ = fluid density

D = pipe diameter

g_c = gravitational constant

Assume the pipes are running full of liquid and the fluid is incompressible. Then

$$m = \rho v A \qquad\qquad (4.2)$$

where

m = mass flow rate

ρ = fluid density

v = average velocity

A = cross sectional area

The pressure change due to elevation difference is given by

$$\Delta P_E = (E_O - E_T) \frac{g\rho}{g_c} \qquad\qquad (4.3)$$

where

E_O = elevation at origin of pipe

E_T = elevation at termination of pipe

ρ = fluid density

g = local gravitational acceleration

g_c = gravitational constant

ΔP_E = pressure drop due to elevation change

Two conservation principles similar to Kirchhoff's node and loop laws apply to hydraulic networks. These are:

Hydraulic node law

$$\sum m_{in} = \sum m_{out} \qquad\qquad (4.4)$$

where

$\sum m_{in}$ = sum of mass flows coming into junction

$\sum m_{out}$ = sum of mass flows leaving junction

Hydraulic loop law

$$\sum_i \Delta P_i = 0 \qquad\qquad (4.5)$$

where

$\sum_i \Delta P_i$ = the algebraic sum of the pressure drops around a single loop

4.2.2 Start Simple—Work Up to Complex

Every engineer who has had an elementary course in circuit analysis has been formally exposed to this process. The performance equations of the individual elements, i.e., resistor, capacitor, and inductor, are given. Relationships regarding how these elements interact, namely the conservation laws known as Kirchhoff's current law and Kirchhoff's voltage law are presented. Finally, complex circuits are modeled by simultaneously applying the necessary performance equations and the relationships governing interactions among or between the individual elements. The combined collection of equations represents a model that could be used to simulate the performance of the entire circuit.

This exact process can be generalized and applied to a wide variety of problems. There are some items of concern to modelers which are not usually covered in elementary courses. These include: under what conditions do the performance equations apply, i.e., what is the envelope of applicability; how they change outside of the envelope of applicability; and how much error is involved in using them for extrapolating outside of the envelope of applicability. Consideration must be given to answering how the model should respond to out of range inputs. Should it abort or use some default value and try to continue. The answers to such questions must be supplied as necessary when the predicted performance does not match actual performance.

Using Equations 4.1 and 4.2, a model of the network can be developed consisting of a system of equations. The unknowns in the equations are m, v, and ΔP. So far, for our example, there are 22 equations (11 like Equation 4.1 and 11 like Equation 4.2) and 33 unknowns. However, the velocities, v, can be represented in terms of the mass flow rates from Equation 4.2 and the result substituted into Equation 4.1 resulting in a simplification.

Solving for v from Equation 4.2

$$v = \frac{m}{\rho A}$$

Substituting into Equation 4.1 gives

$$\Delta P = \frac{fLm^2}{2\pi \rho D^5 g_c} \qquad\qquad (4.6)$$

Now there are only 11 equations and 22 unknowns. Equations of the form of 4.3 have no unknowns in them since the elevation at each end of a section of pipe are known.

Since there are nine junctions, Equation 4.4 can be used to generate nine more equations with no new unknowns, for a total of 20 equations and 22 unknowns. Two other independent relationships are needed. These are provided by the hydraulic loop law, Equation 4.5.

Looking at the diagram of the network (Figure 3.1), there are three loops. Define loop I as containing pipes #1, 2, 3, and 4; loop II as pipes #4, 5, 6, 7, 8, and 11; and loop III as pipes #7, 9, and 10.

For loop I,

$$\Delta P_1 + \Delta P_2 + \Delta P_3 + \Delta P_4 = 0 \qquad\qquad (4.7a)$$

For loop II,

$$\Delta P_4 + \Delta P_5 + \Delta P_6 + \Delta P_7 + \Delta P_8 + \Delta P_{11} = 0 \qquad\qquad (4.7b)$$

For the triangular loop,

$$\Delta P_7 + \Delta P_9 + \Delta P_{10} = 0 \qquad\qquad (4.7c)$$

But now there are 23 equations and only 22 unknowns. As it turns out, only eight of the nine equations like Equation 4.4 can be independent.

Suppose the flow-splits at each junction starting from the left have been made except for junctions 6-7-10, 7-8-9, and 9-10. When the splits are calculated for junctions 6-7-10 and 7-8-9, the flows in pipes #9 and 10 will already be determined, leaving only the double check: does $m_9 + m_{10}$ = external flow at junction 9-10.

The set of equations is now complete, with 22 equations and 22 unknowns. If we had a procedure for solving simultaneous nonlinear equations, theoretically, the problem is solved.

4.2.3 Iterate

Iterate is an intransitive verb meaning to try again, preferably after a modification. The schematic of the modeling process given in

Figure 2.1 clearly indicates the major potential loops in the modeling process. Within any of the process blocks depicted, there can be smaller iteration loops. Computer modeling, for instance, consists of producing a result, comparing it to expected results from a known case, and improving the model until the match is satisfactory. Rarely does the first attempt at modeling prove to be completely satisfactory and insusceptible to improvements. Even at the conclusion of the most successful software projects, the authors always have the attitude: if it were to be done again, it should be done differently, in this better way. Modeling is adapting. Modeling is learning. Iterative improvement is the essence of the modeling process.

We left the mathematical model for the hydraulic network as a set of 22 equations and 22 unknowns, based upon Equation 4.1–4.5. Further investigation of the use of these equations uncovers some potential difficulties.

Suppose the external flow into junction 1-2 is 800 (neglecting the units for now). If the flow in pipe #1 is 600, away from junction 1-2, then the flow in pipe #2 is 200, away from junction 1-2. Assuming algebraic signs for the flow rates are given relative to the junction, then

$$m_{in} = 800$$
$$m_1 = -600$$
$$m_2 = -200$$

where a positive number indicates flow toward the junction and a negative sign indicates flow away from the junction.

Note immediately that if the negative sign for the flow in pipe #2 relative to junction 1-2 is correct, the same flow in pipe #2 relative to junction 2-3 must be positive. To compound the problem, assume that loop I has flows as shown in Loop I, and assume for the moment that the pressure drops are positive in the direction of flow. Equation 4.7a requires that summing ΔPs around the loop gives an algebraic total of zero. All clockwise flows should then be considered positive and all counterclockwise negative, i.e., ΔP_1 and ΔP_2 should have the same signs as m_1 and m_2, respectively. Hence, for Loop I, ΔP_1 and ΔP_2 must have opposite signs for use in Equation 4.7a, but must have the same signs for use in Equation 4.4. Furthermore, flow m_4 is clockwise in loop I but counterclockwise in loop II. Clearly, some additional conventions and bookkeeping will be required.

An alternative to numbering each pipe is to number the junctions where two or more pipes meet. Each such junction will be called a node and a number assigned to it arbitrarily. Figure 4.1 shows the network with the node numbers. The pipes can then be

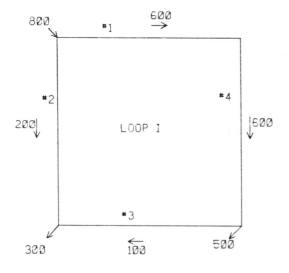

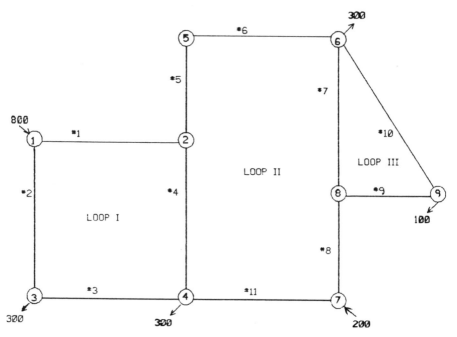

Figure 4.1 Network node numbers.

referred to by their terminal nodes so that what was pipe #1 in Figure 4.1 could now also be referred to as pipe 1-2. The complete table of corresponding nomenclatures is given below.

Fig. 3.1 pipe #	Fig. 4.1 pipe #	Fig. 3.1 node #	Fig. 4.1 node #
1	1-2	1-2	1
2	1-3	1-4-5	2
3	3-4	2-3	3
4	2-4	3-4-11	4
5	2-5	5-6	5
6	5-6	6-7-10	6
7	6-8	8-11	7
8	7-8	7-8-9	8
9	8-9	9-10	9
10	6-9		
11	4-7		

The direction of flow in a pipe could be arbitrarily assumed to be positive in going from the low node number to the high one. If in reality the flow is in the opposite direction, it would simply turn out to be a negative number.

With this node convention and using Equation 4.6 in place of Equations 4.1 and 4.2, the complete set of equations can now be rewritten.

Pressure drops:

$$\Delta P_{1-2} = \frac{8 \, f \, L_{1-2} \, m_{1-2}^2}{2\pi^2 g_c D^5 \rho} \tag{4.8a}$$

$$\Delta P_{1-3} = \frac{8 \, f \, L_{1-3} \, m_{1-3}^2}{2\pi^2 g_c D^5 \rho} \tag{4.8b}$$

$$\Delta P_{4-7} = \frac{8 \, f \, L_{4-7} \, m_{4-7}^2}{2\pi^2 g_c D^5 \rho} \tag{4.8c}$$

Node law equations:

$$EF_1 - m_{1-2} - m_{1-3} = 0 \tag{4.9a}$$

$$m_{1-2} - m_{2-5} - m_{2-4} = 0 \tag{4.9b}$$

$$m_{1-3} - m_{3-4} - EF_3 = 0 \tag{4.9c}$$

$$-EF_4 + m_{3-4} + m_{2-4} - m_{4-7} = 0 \tag{4.9d}$$

$$m_{2-5} - m_{5-6} = 0 \tag{4.9e}$$

$$m_{5-6} - EF_6 - m_{6-8} - m_{6-9} = 0 \tag{4.9f}$$

$$EF_7 + m_{4-7} - m_{7-8} = 0 \tag{4.9g}$$

$$m_{7-8} + m_{6-8} - m_{8-9} = 0 \tag{4.9h}$$

Loop law equations:

$$\Delta P_{1-2} + \Delta P_{2-4} - \Delta P_{3-4} - \Delta P_{1-3} = 0 \tag{4.10a}$$

$$\Delta P_{2-5} + \Delta P_{5-6} + \Delta P_{6-8} - \Delta P_{7-8} - \Delta P_{4-7} - \Delta P_{2-4} \tag{4.10b}$$
$$= 0$$

$$\Delta P_{6-9} - \Delta P_{8-9} - \Delta P_{6-8} = 0 \tag{4.10c}$$

4.2.4 Develop Large Models Modularly

The example of the complex electrical circuit mentioned above epito-
mizes this principle. Individual elements or parts of a system can
usually be modeled. The models of these individual elements should
be tested for their suitability before inclusion in a network of interacting members. What usually remains is to develop relationships describing the interactions between various members. The principle of
conservation can often be applied fruitfully to this area, as it was
by Kirchhoff in the case of electrical circuit networks.

The overall network modeling equations are given as Equations
4.8, 4.9, and 4.10. However, there remains the calculation of
f, the Moody friction factor in Equation 4.8. It can be obtained
for hand calculations from the Moody diagram [11]. Graphs are
not convenient for computer models. Fortunately, considerable
attention has been devoted to developing equations specifically
for calculating f on the computer [12,13]. The equations below,

due to Churchill [15], are relatively convenient to use because they cover the entire range of Reynolds numbers of practical interest.

$$A = \left[2.457 \ Ln \left(\cfrac{1}{\left(\cfrac{7}{Re}\right)^{0.9} + .27\left(\cfrac{\varepsilon}{D}\right)} \right) \right]^{16} \qquad (4.11)$$

$$B = \left(\frac{37530}{Re}\right)^{16} \qquad (4.12)$$

$$f = 8 \left[\left(\frac{8}{Re}\right)^{12} + (A + B)^{-3/2} \right]^{1/12} \qquad (4.13)$$

where Re is the Reynolds number given by

$$Re = \frac{4m}{\pi \mu D} \qquad (4.14)$$

where ε is pipe roughness in feet, and μ is fluid viscosity in centipoise.

During the development of the computer program, the calculation of the friction factor naturally lends itself to being one module of the model. A general friction factor subroutine can be written and checked out quite independently, with no regard to the specific hydraulic network problem.

4.2.5 Model Only Those Characteristics Necessary

Developing equations which adequately represent the system under study is somewhat of an art. Many aspects of systems might be described by equations and logic rules, but not all of these aspects will necessarily contribute to getting adequate performance from the model. Any superfluous entities included in the model might result in the following consequences: (1) wasting time in developing the equations, (2) obscuring more vital features, (3) distracting the analysis because of extra details of input and output, and (4) producing inefficient execution of the model at simulation time. Good engineering judgment will be required to include what is necessary and at the same time exclude what is not necessary.

Once calculated results from the model are available, they can be used to determine the sensitivity of the results to the inclusion or exclusion of various features. Here again, the iterative nature of the process of model development and the advantages of modular construction are evident.

To put things in perspective relative to the hydraulic network problem, recall that the problem statement was given, then refined somewhat. Next, a mathematical model was developed. Due to certain nomenclatural problems, another iteration in the analysis phase was necessary to get a degree of simplification and a consistent set of n-simultaneous equations in n unknowns.

Unfortunately, some of the equations are nonlinear so the powerful tools from linear algebra will not be sufficient to find the solution. Some general methods for solving nonlinear equations will be discussed in Chapter 5. However, because they are general methods, they do not take into consideration the special form of the set of equations of the hydraulic network. They are thus not particularly efficient even if they do converge to a solution, something that is not guaranteed.

There are two gross steps of concern here: (1) to develop the model equations, and (2) to find an efficient and robust technique for solving the equations. Further investigation of solution techniques will yield a method modified from the one proposed by Hardy Cross which is reportedly both efficient and robust.

The problem has been defined, analyzed, modeled, and analyzed some more until some potentially viable solution procedures were found. The next steps will be to refine the solution procedure, then to solve the model equations.

4.2.6 Make Assumptions or Hypotheses

If the behavior of a system were well understood and easily predicted, it wouldn't be necessary to go to the trouble of producing a computer model of it. Since there must be something about the system behavior that is unknown or poorly understood, it will usually be true that assumptions about the causes must be made. These assumptions should be clearly identified and stated so that if the model and real system performances don't coincide in the important aspects under study, different assumptions can be put forth and subsequently tested. Iteration is inevitable. The trick is to identify the processes which are not being modeled well and to improve the pertinent modules of the model.

Major assumptions about the hydraulic network were:

1. Only steady-state analysis is to be considered

2. Fluid properties are constant

These simplifying assumptions greatly reduce the effort required for developing a mathematical model. Algebraic equations are, in general, easier to solve than differential equations. Thus, the first assumption is significant in both model development time and solution time.

If the fluid properties don't remain substantially constant, either some table with an accompanying interpolation procedure or some equation of state which will produce the properties as a function of the appropriate variables will be required.

4.2.7 State Constraints

Constraints are often overlooked or ignored in discussions of system performance. The models running around in the "experts" heads usually overlook different constraints and lead to the verbal disagreements about how a system will perform under certain conditions. If the system is nonlinear in behavior or if two or more constraints can be active simultaneously, intuition and hunches are inadequate and often misleading. The more complex a system is, the more likely it is that the system will operate at or near one or more constraints and perform in a nonintuitive way.

Constraints can be physical, operational, or political. Physical constraints are due to physical limitations: the volume of liquid a vessel can hold is limited by its size; the maximum voltage across an element in a circuit is limited by the voltage source; etc. Operational constraints are set by the operators of the system because of performance considerations. These might be associated with safety—such as maximum temperature in a furnace, a maximum rpm in an engine—or desire for efficient use of the equipment—such as driving a car between 45 and 55 mph to get good gasoline mileage, or leaving an electrical component on continuously to extend it operational life (where cycling on and off is detrimental as is the case of light bulbs). Political constraints are usually also operational in nature, but are more for compromise than for efficiency or longevity. An example would be the throughput of a joint-venture plant where one partner is interested in maximum throughput and the other in lowest cost per unit produced. Since these two policies might be mutually exclusive, some compromise is arrived at and provides a real constraint on how to operate the plant.

The hydraulic network example presents no obvious constraints that affect the modeling. The pipes will be designed for some operating pressure range and specified as schedule 40, pvc, etc. That these specifications are sufficient and do not represent design overkill can be investigated using the model. If, say, some section of pipe were old and pitted, and for safety considerations the plant operators decided the pressure in that segment of piping should not exceed a certain level, then the model could be extended to investigate the effects of valve settings and pump rates on pressure so that the desired quantities of water could be delivered elsewhere in the system while maintaining low pressure in the old pitted section.

4.2.8 Alternate Top-Down and Bottom-Up Approach

In the top-down approach, the overall objectives are stated. These should be in enough detail to allow the actual programmers to determine whether the code they are producing is actually accomplishing one or more of the objectives. The bottom-up approach takes details of what is desired by the persons who are actually going to use the system. These two inputs are rationalized as the system definition is refined in such a way as to meet the objectives set by the "upper management," and at the same time, perform as much as possible of those items given by the intended actual users.

The boss wants to perform "what if" studies for locating new additions. The operators of the water main system are interested in discovering disparities between theoretical calculations and actual data which might help them anticipate problems and isolate changes such as plugging, excessive scale deposits, or significant leaks.

4.3 MODEL CONSTRUCTION

There is an intimate relationship for any system being modeled between causes and effects, inputs and outputs, and system variables. A good model will use major variables to represent the causes and effects and be able to at least generate approximate outputs from known inputs. The trick is to discover the significant variables and formulate reasonably simple relationships which behave enough like the system to make the model useful.

Creativity, insight, experience, and intuition all play major parts in model building. Hence, it is not possible to present a complete, absolutely foolproof way to develop a model. It is probably not even desirable to reduce model development to some unalterable recipe since that would tend to stifle creativity, which must always come to bear during the generation of a model. However, the outlines of some methodological structure can be given to help guide the process and perhaps stimulate original but organized thinking. These structures are progressively vaguer from Section 4.3.1 to 4.3.5, requiring more work and imagination on the part of the modeler.

4.3.1 Obvious Structure Least vague

The relationships connecting effects to causes in this kind of structure are known. Under these circumstances, it is a fairly straightforward process to prepare a model. An example of this might be a two-phase flash unit for an oil-gathering system. Knowing the incoming composition, pressure, and temperature, the split of vapor and liquid can be determined. The relationships between vapor-liquid equilibrium, composition, and operating conditions are known. The hydraulic network being presented is another example of a system having an obvious cause and effect structure.

4.3.2 Analogous Structure

In this kind of structure, the actions of the causes on the system generate effects in a manner similar to some totally unrelated system. How the system converts inputs into outputs is not clear, but by using the analog as a model, the behavior of the undetermined system relationships can be approximated.

Forrester [15,16] used classical feedback control loops as a useful analog to describe the behavior of segments of society in his books on industrial dynamics and urban dynamics. The apparently successful use of this analogy lead to its controversial application reported in "Limits to Growth" [17].

4.3.3 Excess Information Structure

Here, there are a multitude of inputs and outputs and variables which can affect the system. The linking relationships are not known well and, furthermore, it is not known which are the major variables. Data collection and analysis will have to be done before any model can be developed. Experimentation with various hypothetical combinations of relationships will help determine the major variables. Sometimes, the myriad variables can be related to one or two significant variables, greatly simplifying further analysis and modeling.

One feasible approach that has been used is to include all possible variables in a multiple linear regression analysis. However, this "shotgun" approach has two severe drawbacks. The most important defect is that it usually doesn't lead to any significant new insights about what the really important variables are. The other major shortcoming of this approach is that any such model should not be used for extrapolation, which is an activity that the boss always expects. In short, the prize is usually not worth the game, at least not at this stage. Any new variables or changes in the system render the old regression equations unreliable.

4.3.4 Insufficient Data Structure

In this situation, the cause-effect relationships cannot be isolated
from existing operating data. A typical example of this type might
be a manufacturing plant which keeps records on raw materials, operating conditions, and products. These are all things managers are
interested in, but the collected data do not permit the correlation of
cause and effect. The plant has been collecting data useful to it for
standard operational purposes, but they will not yield a model which
can be used to study some projected change such as increased capacity, change in feedstock, or change in a catalyst in a reactor.

The essential feature of developing a useful model for this type
of situation is experimentation. Planned experiments, based upon
the design of experiments concepts will facilitate the collection of the
data required and help organize the results.

4.3.5 Nebulous Structure

Here, data about cause and effect, input and output, and internal
system variables are not available and not attainable. A nuclear fus-
sion reaction might be an example. That doesn't mean the case is
completely hopeless. Hypotheses can still be set forth. These should
follow the course advocated throughout this book of starting simple
and adding complexity in stages. Then, some type of experiment, not
usually involving the entire real system, is devised to check general
trends in the model in quantitative terms. Successive waves of dis-
aggregation, hypothesizing, experimentation, aggregation, and analysis follow one after the other with the additional knowledge about the
system gained on each iteration.

The preceeding discussion except for the material specifically per-
taining to the hydraulic network, applies generally to mathematical and
computer modeling of all kinds. There is, however, a bifurcation in
model categories depending primarily upon how certainly the effects are
related to the causes. These two categories of systems can be referred
to as: (1) deterministic systems, and (2) probabilistic or stochastic
systems. Since the approaches to modeling these two classes of systems
are so different, as are the resulting model structures, they will be
discussed separately.

4.4 DETERMINISTIC SYSTEMS

A deterministic system is one in which chance or probability plays no
part. That means that, for a given model, once the inputs are known,
the outputs can be determined. Examples of such systems are familiar
to most engineers from current work or past academic training. These
deterministic models consist largely of conservation laws and performance equations from the various engineering disciplines.

The hydraulic network has been modeled as a deterministic system. In general, systems in this category are somewhat easier to
model than stochastic ones. The starting place for deterministic system models can be found in the physical sciences: examples include
the conservation of mass, energy, and momentum principles; thermo-
dynamics; and the many empirical or semiempirical performance equations, such as Hooke's spring law, Ohm's law of resistance, and the
Darcy pressure drop equation—all familiar to most engineers.

Each engineering discipline has its sources of equations, charts,
and tables to provide a rich variety of starting blocks for modeling.
These familiar building blocks can be joined together to successfully
model systems of a complexity ranging from simple to immensely complex.

As indicated in Chapter 2, the steady-state aspects of a system
can be modeled, or the dynamic aspects. Normally, it is easier to both
generate the model and solve it for the steady-state case. However,
if the essence of what needs to be simulated involves variations with
time and/or some spatial dimension, then a model of system dynamics
must be the result.

There is a fine semantic distinction between dynamic models and
models of dynamics: the former possibly indicates that the model itself is changing in response to some system condition or is being periodically updated, such as in some evolutionary operation (EVOP) control models; while the latter clearly means the system changes with
time and the model reflects these changes. The material in this book
will deal only with models of dynamics, but will use either phrase to
refer to such models.

Since modeling system dynamics involves setting up and solving
differential equations, the solution procedures for the mathematics
will be somewhat more involved. These will be discussed in Chapter 5.
The short example below will illustrate the modeling process and the
resulting differential equations.

Example 4.1

An ideal mixing tank is one in which the material entering the tank is
assumed to be instantaneously mixed and one in which the concentration within the tank is homogeneous. For such a tank, at any instant,
the concentration in the outlet is equal to the concentration in the
tank itself. Figure 4.2 represents an ideal mixing tank having a concentration of C_z in the tank at some time zero, and having an inlet
stream of known concentration C_i suddenly start adding material to
the tank. At the same time, the outlet stream begins to flow so that
the volume in the tank remains constant. How can this simple mixer
be modeled? Begin by applying the conservation of mass principle to
the tank, considering the tank to be the system

Rate in − rate out = rate of accumulation

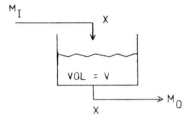

Figure 4.2 Simple mixing tank.

For a nonreacting two-component system, say materials A and B, apply the conservation of mass to component A

$$m(A_i) - m(A_0) = m(A_{sys})$$

What is $m(A_{sys})$, the mass of A in the system, at any time? In terms of concentration, $C(A)$, which has units of lb/ft^3

$$m(A_{sys}) = VC(A_{sys})$$

where V is the volume of the tank. Then, differentiating with respect to time

$$\frac{dm(A_{sys})}{dt} = \frac{V \; dC(A)}{dt}$$

If the incoming stream is flowing steadily at Q ft^3/hr then

$$m(A_i) = QC(A_i)$$

where $C(A_i)$ is the concentration of A coming into the tank. Similarly, since the volume in the tank is not changing

$$Q_{out} = Q_{in} = Q$$

$$m(A_0) = QC(A_0)$$

Now the concentration of the outlet stream at any instant is equal to the concentration in the tank, hence

$$m(A_0) = QC(A_{sys})$$

Combining these relationships gives

$$QC(A_i) - QC(A_{sys}) = V \frac{dC(A_{sys})}{dt}$$

or

$$\frac{dC(A_{sys})}{dt} = \frac{Q}{V}[C(A_i) - C(A_{sys})]$$

This last equation is a model in terms of the single unknown variable $C(A_{sys})$. In it, Q/V represents a capacitive effect for fluid systems much as C does for electrical ones. Given numeric values for the pertinent system parameters, the equation can now be solved either analytically or numerically.

4.5 STOCHASTIC SYSTEMS

Stochastic systems can have continuous variables, discrete variables, or a mixture of both. A wide variety of these sytems can be modeled using what are generically referred to as discrete-event simulators. The material in this book will limit itself to this type of system. Several software packages are available which are general discrete-event simulators. A partial list of some of the more widely used packages includes: GPSS [1], SIMULA [2], SIMSCRIPT [3], and GASP [4]. In addition to the general packages, many specific application oriented programs exist also.

In the literature of business administration and management science, references to simulation activities and software invariably refer to stochastic simulation. For the authors and readers in this segment of the population, the term simulation is synonymous with stochastic simulation. Readers from engineering and scientific backgrounds should be aware of this limited connotation.

A discrete-event simulator must be capable of two fundamental things:

1. Keeping track of multiple entities and activities

2. Generating and using random (or pseudorandom) distributions

Capability 1 can be further broken down into the following:

(a) *Representing the various entities in a system.* The entities will have some special characteristics or attributes which are

of interest in the simulation, such as capacity or time to
perform an action.

(b) *Manipulating the entities.* This might be individually or in
sets. Assigning and using priorities is sometimes important.
Various queue disciplines such as first in—first out (FIFO),
or last in—first out (LIFO) are frequently employed.

(c) *Scheduling the activities.* Keeping track of the time of occurrence of various actions is always necessary. There are
two basic approaches to keeping track of time: (1) incremental marching, and (2) event triggering. Marching
through time in constant time increments is the easiest to
implement and understand. However, if there are wide disparities in the times between successive events, marching
can be very inefficient.

When the events are used to trigger jumps in time, the
execution is more efficient, but the software is more difficult to develop and the results are more difficult to debug.
To a user, the ease of simulation is about the same for either
approach. Selection of a method then boils down to considerations of convenience or availability, and efficiency of
execution. To a software system developer, selection of
the approach method reduces to the classical trade-offs between the time of software development and the execution
efficiency of the final product.

Unless there are special circumstances warranting it,
writing a discrete-event simulation program without using
one of the available languages would be somewhat like writing a FORTRAN compiler to solve a set of equations.

(d) *Collecting and reporting results.* Relevant statistics are
collected and reported. Graphical output such as histo-
grams and other distributions enhance the visual impact
and effectiveness of the reports.

Capability 2 usually depends heavily on the generation of pseudo-
random numbers which is discussed next in some detail.

4.5.1 Pseudo-Random Numbers

At the heart of every stochastic model is some technique for generating
random numbers. These techniques vary from using white noise signal
pickers to doing table look up to using mathematical formulas. Signal
pickers are special hardware and are not always available. That leaves
table look up and the use of formulas. Table look up is satisfactory for
limited applications but can present tedious data entry tasks for larger
problems. There remains the use of mathematical formulas.

The theory of numbers provides several iterative procedures for generating a sequence of numbers which is nonrepeating—but only for a while. Eventually each of these sequences duplicates a number and the sequence repeats from there on. The secret is to produce a sequence with the following attributes:

1. Relatively long sequences

2. Gives good measures of stochasticity, i.e., statistical properties of randomness

3. Can readily be generated on the computer

Because of attribute 1, i.e., there can be lots of numbers generated, and attribute 2, the sequence behaves like a bunch of random numbers as far as shown by several statistical properties [7], the numbers in these sequences are referred to as pseudo-random numbers. They are not truly random because each sequence eventually repeats itself, but for all practical purposes they suffice.

Some of the commercially available discrete-event simulators do a better job of satisfying the measures of stochasticity than others [5]. The two basic measures of stochasticity are the chi-squared test for uniformity and tests for independence.

Since the production of pseudo-random numbers is so important to the simulation of stochastic processes, one representative technique will be discussed to give the flavor of what is behind all stochastic simulations.

Lehmer's Multiplicative Congruential Method [6,8]   RND

The basic recursive algorithm for this method is

$$N_{j+1} = rN_j \ (\text{mod } p) \tag{4.15}$$

where

N_j = A pseudo-random number on the jth iteration

N_{j+1} = A pseudo-random number on the j + 1st iteration

p = A large prime number

r = A primitive root of p with a relatively large number of digits

N_0, called the seed, starts the sequence and can be varied to get different sequences. If p and r are selected as indicated, this method is guaranteed to produce p-1 numbers in the sequence before repeating starts. However, the process of determining p and r, while theoretically simple, is not straightforward numerically due to the finite length of computer words.

A primitive root, r, of integer p, is an integer, the order of which is the number of positive integers less than and prime to p. The integers a and b are relatively prime if the greatest common divisor of a and b is 1. This is indicated symbolically by

$$(a,b) = 1$$

The order of r(mod p) is the least positive exponent, x, such that $r^x = 1 \pmod{p}$, or $r^x \pmod{p} = 1$. Mod is short for modulo. A(mod b) = the remainder of a/b. Thus 9(mod 5) = 4.

For example, suppose p = 7 and r = 3. Both are prime numbers and hence r and p are relatively prime (although it is not required for either of them to be prime for them to be relatively prime). To find the order of r, calculate

r = 3, then 3(mod 7) = 3

r^2 = 9, then 9(mod 7) = 2

r^3 = 27, then 27(mod 7) = 6

r^4 = 81, then 81(mod 7) = 4

r^5 = 243, then 243(mod 7) = 5

r^6 = 729, then 729(mod 7) = 1

By the definition of order, x = 6, the order of 3(mod 7) is 6. The positive integers less than and prime to 7 are:

1, 2, 3, 4, 5, 6

Therefore, 3 is a primitive root of 7.

Using p = 7 and r = 3, one would expect a cycle from Lehmer's multiplicative method of length 6. Let N_0 = 2, for r = 3, p = 7, then

$N_1 = (3 \cdot 2)(mod\ 7) = 6$

$N_2 = (3 \cdot 6)(mod\ 7) = 4$

$N_3 = (3 \cdot 4)(mod\ 7) = 5$

$N_4 = (3 \cdot 5)(mod\ 7) = 1$

$N_5 = (3 \cdot 1)(mod\ 7) = 3$

$N_6 = (3 \cdot 3)(mod\ 7) = 2 = N_0$

So the cycle starts again. As predicted, since 3 is a primitive root of $p = 7$, and the order of 3(mod 7) is 6, there are $p - 1 = 6$ numbers in the calculated sequence.

By contrast, suppose $r = 2$ and $p = 7$. Let $N_0 = 3$. Then

$$N_1 = (2 \cdot 3)(\text{mod } 7) = 6$$
$$N_2 = (2 \cdot 6)(\text{mod } 7) = 5$$
$$N_3 = (2 \cdot 5)(\text{mod } 7) = 3 = N_0$$

Note the cycle length is only 3 and not 6. That indicates that 2 is not a primitive root of 7.

The number of positive integers less than and prime to integer I can be predicted if the prime factorization of I is known. Suppose the prime factorization of I is given by

$$I = \prod_{i=1}^{n} P_i \qquad (4.16)$$

where P_i is a prime number, and n is the number of different primes in the factorization. Then the number of positive integers less than and prime to I is given by

$$NLP(I) = \prod_{i=2}^{n} (P_i - 1) \, P_i^{x_i - 1} \qquad (4.17)$$

where NLP is the number of positive integers less than and prime to I, and x_i is the exponent for prime P_i. Note the index i starts at 2 since the prime number 1 is excluded from the calculation for NLP.

Example 4.2

Suppose $I = 7$. Then the prime factorization for 7 is

$$I = 1 \cdot 7$$

and hence

$$NLP(7) = (7 - 1) \, 7^{(1-1)} = 6$$

which was established in the paragraphs above.

Example 4.3

As further illucidation, suppose $I = 6$. The prime factorization of I is then

$I = 1 \cdot 2 \cdot 3$

For which integer

$$NLP(6) = (2 - 1) \; 2^0 \cdot (3 - 1) \; 3^0 = 2$$

The integers less than and prime to 6 are 1 and 5. The numbers 2, 3, and 4 are excluded because the greatest common divisor between them and $I = 6$ is not equal to 1, and hence they are not relatively prime to 6. Calculating NLP(I) requires that the prime factorization of I be determined. This is not always easy to do for large numbers, although algorithms do exist [9].

Quick and Dirty Method

If it is not convenient to determine a large prime and one of its primitive roots to use in Lehmer's method described above, Mize and Cox [8] give a technique for use with binary computers. For a computer with b binary bits in a word, they recommend choosing

$$p = 2^b \qquad\qquad\qquad (4.18)$$

$r = 8t + 3$ (to make it odd)

$t =$ any integer

$N_0 =$ any odd number

However, since 2^b is not a prime number, but is in fact an even number, and choosing $r = 8t + 3$ does not guarantee that p and r are relatively prime and certainly does not guarantee that r is a primitive root of p, this method can and frequently does produce sequences with extremely short cycle lengths.

Example 4.4

Suppose the computer word had only 6 bits. Then $b = 6$ so that using the quick method

$$p = 2^6 = 64$$

Let $t = 7$, and by Equation 4.18

$$r = 8(7) + 3 = 59$$

As a seed, use

$$N0 = 11$$

Using these data Lehmer's multiplicative congruential method produces the sequence

$$N_1 = (59 \cdot 11)(\bmod\ 64) = 9$$

$$(N_2 \ldots N_{11}) = (19, 33, 27, 57, 35, 17, 43, 41, 51, 1, 59, 25, 3, 49)$$

$$N_{12} = 11 = N_0$$

So the cycle length is 12. However, the largest prime number less than 64 is 61. Therefore, if p were chosen to be 61 and a primitive root of 61 were selected for r, Lehmer's method would produce a sequence of cycle length 60 rather than 12.

If r = 2 for p = 61, a cycle of length 60 is attained. This means that 2 is a primitive root of 61, i.e., $2^{60}(\bmod\ 61) = 1$ and 60 is the smallest power, x, of 2 such that $2^x(\bmod\ 61) = 1$.

Primitive Roots

In theory it is fairly easy to determine if some candidate integer, I, is a primitive root of prime p. The results of

$$r = I^x(\bmod\ p) \tag{4.19}$$

are computed for x = 1 to x = p − 1. If r = 1 only for x = p − 1, then I is a primitive root. However, the straightforward application of the theory is not of much use because of the finite size of computer words. If, for instance, p = 61, as in the example above, the candidate integers would have to be raised to the power 60 to test them using Equation 4.19. And for practical applications, a sequence of less than a few thousand would not be sufficient. Hence if p = 1001, say, the integer candidates for primitive roots would have to be tested by computing I^{1000}.

The numerical problem has thus gotten out of hand. Fortunately, there are other ways of testing the same condition. A residue is the remainder after integer a is divided by integer b and is the result obtained using modulo arithmetic. Notice the sequence of residues of successive powers of 2 with p = 7.

$$r1 = 2(\bmod\ 7) = 2$$

$$r2 = 2^2(\bmod\ 7) = 4$$

$$r3 = 2^3(\bmod\ 7) = 1$$

$$r4 = 2^4(\bmod\ 7) = 2$$

$$r5 = 2^5(\bmod\ 7) = 4$$

etc.

Each successive residue can be computed from the previous residue without ever computing 2^n. Thus

r2 = (r1·2)(mod 7) = 4(mod 7) = 4

r3 = (r2·2)(mod 7) = 8(mod 7) = 1

r4 = (r3·2)(mod 7) = 2(mod 7) = 2

etc.

The same is true for any integer, I, so that the general recursive relationship is

$$r_n = (r_{n-1} \cdot I)(\mathrm{mod}\ p)$$ (4.20)

This recursive relationship allows one to avoid calculating large powers of integers to determine if they are primitive roots or not. The sequence for candidate I is calculated and counted until the first residue that equals 1 is encountered. If the count at that point is equal to NLP(p), the integer I is a primitive root.

4.5.2 Distributions

Generating pseudo-random numbers is the bedrock process for stochastic simulation. On this foundation a superstructure is erected usually involving information about random samples. These samples are described by what statisticians call distribution functions, or just distributions for short. Rather than describing each member of a sample and its properties, some distribution is used to represent the aggregate properties of the population under study.

Many standard distributions are described in any book on statistics [20]. Of these, the most frequently used for modeling are the Poisson, normal, and uniform distributions.

The Poisson distribution is used because it is one of the most mathematically tractable distributions. This distribution is applicable to systems in which some kind of event occurs randomly over time or one or more spatial dimensions. It is the limiting condition to the binomial distribution as the number of items approaches infinity.

Some examples of processes which might be described by a Poisson distribution are: number of defects in a sheet of metal, number of discolored spots on a fruit, and the arrival rate of customers at a bank during a certain part of the day. It has been used many times because its form is simple and it can be analyzed analytically.

The normal distribution is the classic bell-shaped curve that social scientists are so fond of for dealing with human characteristics. Normalcy, then, is some region near the mean value. Variations in

the diameters of shafts manufactured by a certain machine is an example in engineering which can be represented by a normal distribution.
   The most useful distribution for simulation purposes is the uniform distribution. Assume the random variable, x, can take on a
value from the discrete and finite set x_1, x_2, . . . , x_n. Then the
uniform distribution is given by:

$$p(x_i) = \frac{1}{n}$$

   The throw of a single fair die provides a common example. For
the die, the values of x can be 1, 2, . . . , 6 and n is 6. So the
probability of any single number in the set coming up is 1/6. The
distinguishing characteristic of the uniform distribution is that the
probability of the occurrence for each value of the random variable
is the same.
   The cumulative distribution is:

$$F(y) = \sum_{x<y} p(x_i) = \frac{k}{n}$$

where k is the largest number such that x < y. For the single die,
i.e., for y = 3, k = 3, and F(3) = 3/6 = 1/2, the probability that x is
1, 2, or 3 is 1/2.
   Not much detail has been given for the distributions above for
two reasons: (1) they are well explained in any text on statistics,
and (2) real situations tend to have distributions that don't neatly
fit any of the common distributions. But it is of small consequence
because it is relatively easy to represent virtually any real distribution by a transformation involving a uniform distribution. Thus, if
there is an algorithm for calculating numbers uniformly distributed
between, say, 0 and 1, any other distribution can be represented by
first selecting random numbers between 0 and 1 and then using the
transformation to obtain the value of the random variable of interest.
   For example, suppose the length of a standard pipe joint is approximately normally distributed about 8 feet in the following way:

Inches of error	Percent of occurrences
0	2
± .01	66
± .02	30
± .03	2
> .03	0

This manufacturing step is to be simulated on the computer. Every
pipe joint as it is manufactured will have a length assocaited with it.
In the simulation model this could be generated by the following:

Example 4.5

Length = 8 feet + x inches where x is randomly selected using a uniform distribution with numbers between 0 and 1.

Random number	x	Percent of total interval
0−.01	+.03	1
.01−.16	+.02	15
.16−.49	+.01	33
.49−.51	0.0	2
.51−.84	−.01	33
.84−.99	−.02	15
.99−1.0	−.03	1

Thus, by generating a uniform distribution of numbers between 0
and 1 and assigning each random number to a set representing the
actual deviation in size, a good approximation to the empirical distribution of the system being modeled can be represented. This is
sometimes called the inverse transformation method.

For the example above, suppose the first random number generated is 0.21. Then, from the inverse distribution table, the pipe
length would be assumed to be 8 feet + .01 inches. If the random
number were 0.89, then the pipe length would be 8 feet − 0.02 inches.

Such transformations of uniform distributions can be generalized
to correspond to any cumulative distribution. Let the cumulative distribution be denoted $F(x)$. If it is known how to get x from $F(x)$, the
inverse transformation method described above can be used. The
steps are:

1. Generate a random number, r, from a uniform distribution

2. Find the x corresponding to r by using the inverse trans-
    formation, $x = F(r)$

This technique works for any distribution, $F(x)$, which is strictly
increasing.

As a further example, suppose the density function, $f(x)$, is
given by:

x	f(x)
16—50	12
50—75	5
>75	0

Then the cumulative function is

$$F(x) = \int f(x)dx$$

As x goes from 2 to 16, f(x) goes from 0 to 0.765. As x goes from 16 to 75, F(x) goes from 0.765 to 1.0 linearly. The inverse function can be obtained by dividing the interval 0 to 0.765 into 14 equal parts each the length 0.0545 and the interval 0.765 to 1.0 into 59 equal parts of length 0.004. The inverse function would be obtained from the following

Random number	x
0—.0545	2
.0546—.1090	3
.1091—.1636	4
.	
. (14 intervals of length 0.0545)	
.	
.7085—.7630	16
.7631—.7670	17
.7671—.7710	18
.	
. (59 intervals of length 0.004)	
.	
.9961—1.0	75

If tables are not convenient, then algebra can be used to represent the inverse function.

One of the most fruitful applications of stochastic modeling is for risk analysis [19]. The general situation which can be referred to as a risk problem is one which has the following characteristics:

1. There are several possible courses of action.

2. For each course of action there can be alternative outcomes.

3. The probabilities of the alternative outcomes can be estimated.

4. A decisionmaker must choose one of the courses of action.

The decisionmaker's problem, then, is to determine what the possible consequences of each course of action is, how likely each outcome is, and which course will most likely be best for his organization.

In practice, the decisionmaker doesn't do the research to find out probabilities and might not even know the possible consequences of various courses of action [18]. He has some staff gather or prepare the information for him. He remains with a double dilemma: is the data good enough to base a decision on, and what course of action should be chosen? His choice for a course of action might reflect heavily his opinion of whether he thinks the staff has presented a convincing case or not.

The approach to risk analysis is to assign a payoff and a probability of occurrence for each outcome. The expected utility of each choice can then be computed as the sum of the products of each payout times its probability of occurrence. The reasoning then goes that the choice which maximizes the expected utility is the best. This approach works well as long as the outcomes are independent and all possible outcomes can be enumerated.

Risk analysis depends largely upon estimating subjective probability, as opposed to objective probability with which most engineers are familiar. Objective probability is based upon data and observational experience in which occurrences follow some recognizable trends. Subjective probability is based upon opinions or hunches even though these may be educated guesses derived from experience and judgment. The probability of three dots coming up on a fair die is an example of an objective probability. The expectation assigned to striking oil while drilling a rank wildcat illustrates a subjective probability.

REFERENCES

1.   IBM, *GPSS V: Introductory Users Manual*, 2nd ed., New York (1971).
2.   Dahl, O. J., B. Myrhang, K. Nygaard, and G. Birthwhistle, *SIMULA BEGIN*, Petrocelil Charter (1973).
3.   Kiviat, P. J., R. Villanueva, and H. M. Markovitz, *SIMSCRIPT*, Prentice-Hall, Englewood Cliffs, New Jersey (1968).
4.   Kiviat, P. J., and A. Colker, *GASP-A General Activity Simulation Program*, The RAND Corp., P-2864, Santa Monica, California (1964).
5.   Leeming, A. M. C., "A Comparison of Some Discrete-Event Simulation Languages," *SIMULETTER*, 2(1-4):9—16 (1981).
6.   Lehmer, D. H., "Mathematical Methods in Large-Scale Computing Units," *Proc. 2nd Symposium on Large-Scale Digital Calculating Machinery*, Harvard U. Press, Cambridge, Massachussetts, 1951, pp. 141—146.

7. Mize, J. H., and J. G. Cox, *Essentials of Simulation*, Prentice-Hall, Englewood Cliffs, New Jersey, 1968, p. 72.

8. Mize, J. H., and J. G. Cox, *Essentials of Simulation*, Prentice-Hall, Englewood Cliffs, New Jersey, 1968, p. 68.

9. Hutchinson, O. W., "A New Uniform Pseudorandom Number Generator," *Comm. of ACM*, 9(6):432–433 (1966).

10. Akers, L. A., and T. M. Wang, "Simulation of a 3-D Semiconductor Device," *Simulation*, 40(2):43–50 (1983).

11. Brown. G. G., et al., *Unit Operations*, Wiley, New York, 1956, p. 143.

12. Ingels, D. M., *Analysis of Flow in Pipeline Networks*, Masters Thesis, University of Oklahoma, 1962.

13. Olujic, Z., "Compute Friction Factors Fast for Flow in Pipes," *Chem. Eng.*, Dec. 14, 1981, pp. 91–93.

14. Churchill, S. W., *Chem. Eng.*, Nov. 7, 1977, pp. 91–92.

15. Forrester, J. W., *Industrial Dynamics*, MIT Press, Cambridge, Massachusetts, 1961.

16. Forrester, J. W., *Urban Dynamics*, MIT Press, Cambridge, Massachussetts, 1969.

17. Meadows, D., *Limits to Growth*, Club of Rome, 1974.

18. Sagan, C., "Nuclear War and Climatic Catastrophe: Some Implications," *Foreign Affairs*, Winter 1983/84, p. 257.

19. Megill, R. E., *An Introduction to Risk Analysis*, Petrol. Pub. Co., Tulsa, Oklahoma, 1977.

20. Mood, A. M., F. E. Graybill, and C. Boes, *Introduction to the Theory of Statistics*, McGraw-Hill, New York, 1963.

5

SOLVING THE MATHEMATICAL MODEL

Though this be madness, yet there be method in't.

[Shakespeare]

5.1 INTRODUCTION

As mentioned in Chapter 2, writing down a set of equations might constitute a model, but equations are of little use unless they can be solved. The two basic solution approaches are: (1) analytical and (2) numerical. The analytical techniques are more informative and efficient to
use, but much less general in their range of applicability, i.e., it is
common to have equations with no known explicit analytic solution.
These will be left to texts on mathematics [13,14]. Because of their
general usefulness, the material in this book is restricted to a discussion of some useful numerical procedures that are commonly used in
computer simulations.

Two different classes of problems are encountered when modeling systems with sets of equations, whether the equations are linear
or nonlinear. These two categories are:

1. n equations in n unknowns

2. m equations in n unknowns, m < n

with k inequalities in n unknowns, where k can be any number.

If the equations in class 1 problems are independent, they can usually be solved by methods such as those described below. Class 2 problems are solved using optimization techniques, linear programming [1] for linear systems, and nonlinear programming techniques [2,3,7] for nonlinear systems.

5.2 LINEAR ALGEBRAIC SYSTEMS

A set of linear equations can be written as:

$$a_{11}x_1 + a_{12}x_2 + \ldots + a_{1n}x_n = b_1 \qquad (5.1)$$

$$a_{21}x_1 + a_{22}x_2 + \ldots + a_{2n}x_n = b_2$$

.

.

.

$$a_{n1}x_1 + a_{n2}x_2 + \ldots + a_{nn}x_n = b_n$$

where $x_1 \ldots x_n$ are the n unknowns, a_{ij} are known coefficients, and b_i are known constants.

If the number of equations is large, somewhere over four, writing them out explicitly soon becomes tedious and then they are most frequently expressed in array notation in terms of a matrix A and two vectors, x and b.

$$[A]x = b \qquad (5.2)$$

where [A] is an n by n matrix of the coefficients $a_{11} \ldots a_{nn}$, x is an n-membered vector of the unknowns $x_1 \ldots x_n$, and b is an n-membered vector of the right-hand sides (rhs) of 5.1.

There are numerous methods for solving a set of linear equations. These can be broken down into two major categories: (1) direct and (2) indirect. Direct methods are, at least theoretically, finite in the number of operations they take to effect a solution. That is, for n equations there are $O(n)$ operations, where $O(n)$ is some function of n. If there were no problems with roundoff or truncation errors, the number of operations required to solve a set of equations using the direct methods could be calculated directly.

By contrast, the indirect methods approach the solution through successive approximations and theoretically require an indefinite (infinite) number of operations. For the indirect methods to be of any practical value they can't actually take an infinite number of operations. When they converge, they approach the exact answers in a

more or less assymptotic fashion. When the difference between successive approximations is less than some specified tolerance, the indirect methods are considered to have converged on a solution.

From first instincts, it would seem that only direct methods would
ever be of interest. They get directly at the solution in a finite number of operations. But, in fact, there are classes of problems for which
the indirect methods are not only better, but require significantly fewer operations for practical convergence. An important class of these
problems is the solution of sparse matrices.

A sparse matrix is one in which there are few non-zero coefficients in comparison to the zero coefficients. Unless the non-zero
coefficients are banded relatively closely to the diagonal so that one
of the special banding algorithms can be used effectively [5], the number of arithmetic operations to solve a sparse matrix is the same as for
a non-sparse matrix using direct methods. Since the number of operations is roughly proportional to n^3, where n is the number of equations, a matrix of 250 or more rows will require a billion or more
operations.

By contrast, an indirect iteration approach might require only
kn^2 operations per iteration and converge in few enough iterations
that many less total operations are performed; Gauss-Seidel is one
such method [4]. The indirect methods are mentioned here for perspective and will not be addressed further.

5.2.1 Gauss-Jordan

One of the most useful of the direct methods is know as Gaussian
elimination. It is usually effective, although not the most efficient
method. In particular, Gaussian elimination does not take advantage
of any particular structure in the matrix. Such structure as banding,
in which the non-zero coefficients exist only k elements to the right
or left of the diagonal, can be used to advantage in solving sets of
equations with this structure. In particular, matrices with a tri-
diagonal pattern have received considerable attention. Von Rosenberg
[5] presents under one cover specific algorithms for solving tri-
diagonal, penta-diagonal, and general banded matrices. The latter algorithm suffers somewhat from numerical roundoff problems and is only
useful for 32-bit computers when programmed in double precision arithmetic. But these methods do illustrate how the structure can be used
to advantage.

The number of arithmetic operations required by Gaussian elimination for n-simultaneous linear equations is proportional to n^3 [4].

5.2.2 L-U-Decomposition

As noted in Section 5.2.1, Gauss-Jordan is a general method for solving sets of linear equations, but it is not the most efficient method.

In the matrix formulation of the problem, Equation 5.2, the solution can be arrived at by finding A^{-1}, the inverse of matrix A. Then

$$x = A^{-1} b \qquad (5.3)$$

Finding the inverse of matrix A can be done in many ways [6] but one of the most efficient methods is to perform an L-U decomposition on matrix A into an upper triangular matrix B and a lower triangular matrix C such that

$$A = C \cdot B \qquad (5.4)$$

Once the L-U decomposition is found, it is theoretically simple to compute the inverses of matrices B and C and from them, the inverse of A,

$$D = A^{-1} = B^{-1} \cdot C^{-1} \qquad (5.5)$$

However, as it turns out, there are large computational savings involved because the inverses of B and C don't have to be computed to find D. It can be calculated in a very straightforward manner from the elements of B and C. Once the elements for B and C have been determined, the elements of D can be calculated directly from them. The algorithm is described in detail by Faddeeva [6].

To complete the solution once D is found, it remains only to multiply D times the right-hand side, b. This provides another advantage to the matrix formulation. In addition to computational efficiency, it facilitates calculating multiple solutions for different b vectors. Only one multiplication of the matrix D times a particular right-hand-side b vector is required.

The two methods described above, Gauss-Jordan and L-U decomposition, are among the direct methods most frequently used in the computer solution of equations for linear systems. Indirect methods are used for those systems involving sparse, but not banded, coefficient matrices. A user of a simulation package will be indifferent to the solution technique unless large amounts of computation time are involved. In that case, some investigation of the solution procedure used and its computational efficiency relative to other possible procedures might be warranted.

5.3 NONLINEAR ALGEBRAIC SYSTEMS

Linear equations are easy to set up, solve, and analyze compared to nonlinear equations. However, most of the phenomena of the world seem to be nonlinear in nature. Hence, techniques for dealing with nonlinear equations must be found and utilized. One method based on knowing the derivatives of the functions, Newton's method, will be described followed by several methods which do not require explicit knowledge of the derivatives.

In all of the procedures that follow, whether for a single variable or sets of equations, it is required that the functions be well behaved, i.e., be continuous and have continuous derivatives.

5.3.1 Single-Variable Equations

When a model consists of a nonlinear function of a single variable that can be written in the form

$$f(x) = 0 \qquad\qquad (5.6)$$

two approaches to finding a root can be taken, one depending on being able to calculate values of the derivative of the function and one requiring only evaluation of the function itself. One approach requiring derivatives converges as rapidly as any known method, when it works. However, it does not always converge. This method was originally due to Sir Isaac Newton and is referred to by his name. Since Newton's method forms the basis for a large fraction of all root-finding techniques, a brief summary is given below. It is described in detail by Dorn and McCracken [4].

Newton's Method

Given a function of the form

$$f(x) = 0$$

and its derivative

$$\frac{df}{dx} = f'(x)$$

it is possible to guess at the root of $f(x)$ and use the function and its derivative evaluated at the guessed value for x to calculate another guess which will be better than the previous one. The method can be expressed succinctly by

$$x_{k+1} = x_k - f(x_k) \qquad\qquad (5.7)$$

where x_k is the approximation for the root on iteration k, x_{k+1} is the approximation for the root to be used for iteration k + 1, and $f'(x_k)$ is the derivative of the function $f(x)$ on iteration k.

A necessary condition for the method to converge is that the initial guess, x_0, be close enough to the actual root that it falls into a region in which the second derivative, $f''(x)$ does not change sign. If the second derivative is unknown, then it might not be possible to determine the region of convergence. In that case, the progress of the iterations should be closely observed to determine if convergence is being obtained.

If there are multiple roots, as with a polynomial, there is practically no foolproof way to determine which of the roots will be found (if indeed any are) when using Newton's method.

As mentioned earlier, Newton's method requires that one be able to evaluate both the function and its derivative for each iteration. For all practical purposes, that usually means that the analytical expression for the function is explicitly known and is tractable enough to determine an expression for its derivative. For many systems which are functions of one variable, no explicit functional expression is available. This precludes the use of Newton's method.

The Interval-Halving Technique

When the explicit functional form is not known, is known but cannot be solved for x explicitly, or calculating its derivative expression is difficult or not possible, then the function can be treated as a "black box" and solved numerically.

Only a few root-finding procedures guarantee finding a root and then only under certain necessary conditions. Interval halving is assured of succeeding if one simple condition can be met. Suppose the function to be solved is of the form of Equation 5.6:

$$f(x) = 0$$

If the function is continuous and changes signs between XL and XR, then there must be at least one root in the interval between XL and XR. The interval halving method is guaranteed to converge on a root in the interval XL < x < XR under such conditions.

The problem is to bracket the root between some XL and XR. There are no foolproof methods to do this. As a practical contingency, a marching technique can be attempted. The value for x is set to some value, x_{min}. The value of x is then incremented by some step size, Δx, to see if there is a change in the sign of $f(x)$ in going from x to $x + \Delta x$. If there is no change in sign, the process of incrementing x is continued until some maximum value of x, x_{max}, is attained. If no change in sign is found between x_{min} and x_{max}, the value for Δx is decreased and the entire marching process is repeated starting from x_{min} again. Once a root is bracketed between, say, $x(n+1)$ and $x(n)$, the interval-halving technique can be fruitfully applied.

While the method converges under the necessary conditions, it converges more and more slowly as it nears the root.

A more efficient technique using similar logic can be developed from the optimization method known as golden section or the Fibonnaci search from which it derives [7]. Neither of these will be pursued here, but rather an efficient quasi-Newtonian technique called the secant method will be described.

Single-Variable Secant Method

This method, when it converges, it more efficient than the interval-halving procedure. It can be visualized as a numerical approximation to Newton's method. It proceeds iteratively by calculating successive estimates of the slope from two functional evaluations and thus does not require an explicit expression for the derivatives. The method continues by using the latest two values of x and the corresponding values of f(x) to find the next approximation to the root.

Like Newton's method, when it converges, it does so very rapidly, but it is not guaranteed to converge. When writing programs to use these techniques care must be taken to test for convergence within some maximum number of iterations.

It is possible to combine interval-halving and the secant method into one algorithm. Then, if a root is ever bracketed, convergence will be guaranteed, and as long as there is an indication that convergence is happening, the efficient secant method can be used near the root.

5.3.2 Multiple-Variable Nonlinear Algebraic Equations

There is no universal method which is certain to find the roots of all possible sets of nonlinear algebraic equations. But there are a large number of approaches, ranging from the simple expedient of iterative direct substitution to sophisticated heuristic optimization methods. One of the most robust and efficient types of solution procedures is referred to as the quasi-Newton method. Newton's method itself, as applied to multivariable problems by Raphson, can be used if values for the derivatives can be calculated and the functions satisfy all the necessary mathematical conditions of continuity and smoothness. However, this requirement for specific expressions for the derivatives greatly limits its range of applicability, so it will not be discussed further here except to say that, as in the single-variable case, it can suffer from divergence problems—only more severely.

The two quasi-Newton methods to be discussed are the generalized secant method [4] which requires a matrix inversion for each iteration, and a refinement of the secant method due to Broyden [8] which gets around the time-consuming matrix inversion step in a clever way, still retaining the superlinear convergence as the roots are approached.

The price paid for Broyden's efficiency is that it is less robust, i.e., it does not converge for as wide a class of problems.

Multivariable Secant Method

The set of equations to be solved are of the form

$$f1(x_1, \ldots, x_n) = 0 \qquad\qquad (5.8)$$
$$f2(x_2, \ldots, x_n) = 0$$
$$\cdot$$
$$\cdot$$
$$\cdot$$
$$fn(x_1, \ldots, x_n) = 0$$

Since the values of $x1, \ldots, xn$, which are the roots of the functions, are not known initially, some initial guesses must be made. A matrix of differences is defined which is a numerical approximation of the Jacobian. It is used in an iterative equation similar to Equation 5.7. As with the single-variable case, the functions must be evaluated at two points to get the method started.

Like most quasi-Newton methods, if the initial guesses are sufficiently near the roots and the functions are well behaved, the secant method converges rapidly and it can be used where the functions are essentially "black boxes." The vast majority of the computational time is spent evaluating the inverse of the matrix which is a numerical approximation of the Jacobian. Several approaches to avoid inverting the matrix on every iteration have been reported. One of the more useful of these approaches, due to Broyden, is described in the next section.

Any multivariable optimization technique can also be used for root finding. Suppose the functions for which roots are desired are given by Equation 5.8. Then an auxiliary set of equations, shown in Equation 5.9, could also be written.

$$g1(x_1, \ldots, x_n) = f1 \cdot f1 \qquad\qquad (5.9)$$
$$g2(x_1, \ldots, x_n) = f2 \cdot f2$$
$$\cdot$$
$$\cdot$$
$$\cdot$$
$$gn(x_1, \ldots, x_n) = fn \cdot fn$$

and

$$G = g1^2 + g2^2 + \ldots + gn^2 \qquad\qquad (5.10)$$

Equation 5.10 can now theoretically be minimized using any multivariable optimization technique. At the minimum, i.e., when each g is zero, then each f will also be zero.

Broyden's Method [8]

There are two factors which effect the total time it takes for an algorithm to converge to within a stated tolerance: (1) the total number of iterations, and (2) the number of operations per iteration. Broyden devised a procedure to reduce the number of operations per iteration. He did this at the expense of the number of iterations. But, because the reduction in the number of operations was an order of magnitude reduction, the method usually is more efficient than the secant method. For this method it is necessary only to invert a matrix on the first iteration after which the inverse is estimated by a simple calculation. This results in great savings in computation time on succeeding iterations. This decrease in operations per iteration is paid for by some decrease in stability.

The approach taken so far for our network problem is general in that any simple fluid network can be described by the appropriate equations. However, the issue of solving the equations must also be considered. Procedures such as Newton-Raphson iteration and Broyden's method are well-known general methods for solving such systems of equations. However, they take no account of the specific form of the set of equations and are thus not necessarily the most efficient ones to use.

On another level, if a computer program already exists to solve sets of nonlinear equations, it might be an efficient use of manpower to use the "canned" program initially to get answers in the shortest time, trading computer computation time for engineering manpower time.

An Arab aphorism says; "If you can't carry a stone, roll it." The English equivalent is probably, "There is more than one way to skin a cat," not that skinning cats is being advocated. The general principle that applies here is that there are many different ways to solve sets of simultaneous nonlinear equations, some more efficient and some more robust than others. These are discussed above.

Up to now, the hydraulic network has been modeled by 22 simultaneous equations some of which are nonlinear and might cause numerical convergence problems.

However, the procedure for solving the specific equations modeling hydraulic networks has received some attention starting with Hardy Cross [18]. A modified form of the Hardy Cross technique is reportedly most efficient and robust [17,20]. The method takes advantage of the specific structure of the problem, inherently eliminates the sign-convention complications, and generally addresses only the characteristics of the problem that are required for solution. A brief description of the procedure follows:

The network is described as n pipes of known length, diameter, and roughness forming m interconnected loops with various inflows and outflows. The problem is to find how the flows are distributed through the pipes so that the pressure drops are balanced in each loop. For any closed loop, Equation 4.5 must be satisfied. This can be attained by following the four steps given below.

Step 1

The flow in each pipe is arbitrarily assigned, taking into consideration any flows into or out of the system, so that the sum of the flows coming to each node is equal to the sum of the flows leaving each node. This, in essence, forces the network to be in material balance. Signs will be "+" for clockwise flow in a loop and "−" for counterclockwise flow. Flows common to two loops will take the sign of the lowest numbered loop first and then flip-flop signs each time the other loop is being balanced. In practice, almost any distribution that is in material balance can be used, including zero flows where convenient.

Step 2

Using the estimated flow rates, the pressure drops are calculated around each loop in turn. In general, the arbitrary flow distribution will not satisfy Equation 4.5. So, for iteration j, define the sum, $S^{(j)}$, as

$$S^{(j)} = \sum_i \Delta P_i^{(j)} \tag{5.11}$$

Step 3

Calculate a flow correction, Δm, to apply to the flow rates around a loop. This correction should be obtained in such a way as to drive S toward zero on each succeeding iteration.

$$\Delta m = \frac{-\sum \Delta P_i^{(j)}}{\sum R_i^{(j)}} = \frac{-S^{(j)}}{\sum R_i^{(j)}} \tag{5.12}$$

where

$\Delta P_i^{(j)}$ = The pressure drop in pipe i on iteration j

Σ = Clockwise around each loop

$S^{(j)}$ = The sum of pressure drops around a loop

Δm = The mass flow correction to add to the flow in each pipe in a loop

R_i = The correction factor for pipe i given by

$$R = \frac{\partial \Delta P}{\partial m} \qquad (5.13)$$

The details of arriving at Equations 5.12 and 5.13 are described by Ingels and Powers [19].

Step 4

Apply steps 2 and 3 successively to each loop until

$$\sum \left| \Delta m_k \right| \leqslant \varepsilon \qquad (5.14)$$

where

Δm_k = The flow correction for loop k

Σ = The flow correction over all loops

ε = The convergence tolerance, a small positive number

5.4 DIFFERENTIAL EQUATIONS

Models of systems which describe the rate of change of one variable with respect to another contain differential equations. Many analytical techniques exist for finding the solutions of differential equations if they are of a certain form. But just as there are algebraic equations or systems for which analytical techniques are inappropriate or inadequate, so it is with differential equations. No attempt will be made here to discuss analytical techniques. The following discussion will limit itself to two general methods, the Runge-Kutta (R-K) type of explicit method, and one approach to implicit methods.

Explicit methods are those in which each derivative can be broken out and isolated to the left-hand side of an equation and expressed as a function of the other variables. This usually allows an iterative approach. Implicit methods are those in which the equations must be solved simultaneously. The advantages and disadvantages of each will be briefly discussed as the methods are presented.

The numerical solution of differential equations has received much attention. What follows is a mere introduction to some practically useful approaches which could be easily implemented for a wide variety of simulations.

5.4.1 The Runge-Kutta Methods

Numerical solutions of differential equations use one of two approaches: (1) single-step methods, or (2) multistep methods. Most of the latter are referred to as predictor correctors. The Runge-Kutta [4] methods are single-step methods. They all have three distinguishing properties:

1. They are single-step methods.

2. They agree with the Taylor series through some term, Δx^n, where n is called the order of the method.

3. They do not require evaluation of any derivatives, only of the function itself.

Property 3 is what makes the R-K methods of practical value.

As a point of interest, Euler's method is a R-K method of order one (i.e., n = 1 in property 2 above). It is not of much use because it suffers from instability and large truncation errors. The so-called modified Euler or improved Euler methods are order two R-K methods. The fourth-order method is the most commonly used and is often referred to as "the Runge-Kutta method." It is the fourth-order method which is presented next.

The problem is to solve for y given that

$$y' = f(x,y) \qquad\qquad (5.15)$$

$$y(x_0) = y_0 \qquad\qquad (5.16)$$

where

$$y' = \frac{dy}{dx}$$

y_0 = initial condition

The R-K method can be defined by give equations.

$$y_{m+1} = y_m + \frac{\Delta x}{6} (k_1 + 2k_2 + 2k_3 + k_4) \tag{5.17a}$$

$$k_1 = f(x_m, y_m) \tag{5.17b}$$

$$k_2 = f\left(x_m + \frac{\Delta x}{2}, \ y_m + \frac{k_1}{2}\right) \tag{5.17c}$$

$$k_3 = f\left(x_m + \frac{\Delta x}{2}, \ y_m + \frac{k_2}{2}\right) \tag{5.17d}$$

$$k_4 = f(x_m + \Delta x, \ y_m + k_3) \tag{5.17e}$$

where

$$x_{m+1} = x_m + \Delta x$$

$$y_{m+1} = \int_{x_0}^{x_{m+1}} f(x,y) \ dx$$

This fourth-order method, which solves functions of both x and y, is a generalized Simpson's rule which solves functions of x only.

Example 5.1

Suppose the problem to solve is:

$$y' = 3x$$
$$y(0) = 3.$$

The results of using equations 5.17 for $\Delta x = 0.1$ are given in Table 5.1. This compares with the analytical solution of $y(1) = 4.5$.

Equations 5.17a--e are for a single differential equation, but they can be readily extended to multiple equations. Higher-order equations must be reduced to a set of first-order equations in order to use the Runge-Kutta method, but this is easily accomplished as Example 5.2 illustrates.

Example 5.2

Suppose

$$y''' = 3x^2 + y' \tag{a}$$
$$y(0) = 1$$

Table 5.1 Numerical Results of the R-K Method

i	x	y	k1	k2	k3	k4
0	.0	3.0				
1	.1	3.015	.00	.015	.015	.03
2	.2	3.060	.03	.045	.045	.06
3	.3	3.135	.06	.075	.075	.09
4	.4	3.240	.09	.105	.105	.12
5	.5	3.375	.12	.135	.135	.15
6	.6	3.54	.15	.165	.165	.18
7	.7	3.735	.16	.195	.195	.21
8	.8	3.960	.21	.225	.225	.24
9	.9	4.215	.24	.255	.255	.27
10	1.0	4.500	.27	.285	.285	.30

$$y'(0) = 3 \tag{b}$$
$$y''(0) = 0$$

To couch the third-order equation in terms of three first-order equations, a transformation is effected. Let

$$z = y' \text{ and } w = z'$$

then

$$z' = y'' \text{ and } w' = z'' = y'''$$

Equations (a) and (b) can then be written as

$$w' = 3x^2 + z \tag{aa}$$
$$z' = w$$
$$y' = z$$

$$y(0) = 1 \tag{bb}$$
$$z(0) = 3$$
$$w(0) = 0$$

The process of transforming higher-order differential equations into a series of first-order differential equations can be generalized from the above example.

Equations corresponding to 5.17a—e are then needed for multiple-variable equations. The process can be extended and applied to any set of ordinary differential equations.

It is difficult to predict numerical errors when R-K methods are used. But it is known that they suffer from round-off errors and can be numerically unstable for Δx that are either too large or too small.

5.4.2 Implicit Methods for Numerical Integration

The implicit methods are not as convenient to formulate, but have the happy property that they are universally stable and any additional computation per iteration can frequently be compensated for by using a larger time spacing.

Many different implicit methods exist (5). Some are more effective than others for specific classes of problems. The general approach of these methods will be briefly discussed to illustrate the steps involved in solving models involving differential equations.

Suppose the problem is to solve a partial differential equation of the form

$$\frac{\partial^2 y}{\partial x^2} = \frac{\partial y}{\partial t}$$

for x between 0 and 1 where the boundary conditions are:

$y(0,t) = a$ for all t

$y(1,t) = b$ for all t

$y(x,0) = c$ $x < 1$

Consider x to be a spatial dimension which varies between 0 and 1, and the time variable, t, to increase without limit from zero.

One general approach to solving this type problem numerically is to set up a grid as shown in Figure 5.1.

The time axis is divided into increments of size Δt which may be changed as the solution progresses from time zero in the positive t direction. The position along the grid in the t direction can be indicated by the index j. Similarly, the grid spacing in the x direction will be referred to as Δx and will be indexed by i. Any value of the dependent variable, y, at a grid point can be indicated by subscripting with the two indices, e.g., y_{ij}. Since Δx and Δt can take on any values, any value of y in the domain of interest can be denoted.

A finite difference form equivalent to Equation 5.15 is developed for each grid point at a given time level. When the equations for a complete row of the grid, corresponding to time j + 1, are written down,

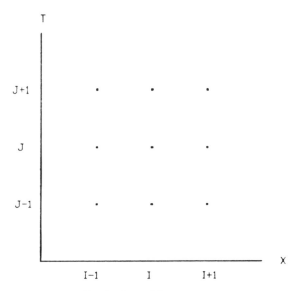

Figure 5.1 Variable grid.

they constitute a set of n-simultaneous linear equations which can be solved using the methods described in Section 5.2. As is common with implicit numerical integration procedures, the complete set of equations at each time step has a specific banded structure which should be recognized so that methods particularly effective for solving systems with that structure can be used to advantage. In the present case, the set of difference equations have a tri-diagonal structure and it would be efficient to employ an algorithm developed specifically for this form [5]. The Crank-Nicolson method, one such implicit technique, is stable for all ratios of Δx and Δt and can thus use relatively large grid spacings. Most texts on numerical methods describe in detail how to set up the requisite difference equations to approximate the various partial derivatives.

To summarize, the differential equations modeling system dynamics or spatial variation can be solved with general numerical procedures which are referred to as explicit or implicit methods. The explicit formulations are easier to set up and program for solution, but have some definite limitations with regard to stability. The implicit methods are numerically stable but require much more effort to program. Combinations of the two approaches are possible and are referred to as mixed explicit-implicit methods.

From a user's point of view, it is evident that implicit methods are preferrable. But from a model developer's point of view, there are trade-offs between guaranteeing stability and computational efficiency versus ease of development.

5.5 IDENTIFYING AND USING SYSTEM STRUCTURE

Systems of interacting parts in which information material, or energy
flows from one part of the system to another can often be decomposed
into subsystems which are easier to analyze. The problem is how to rationally decompose such systems. A branch of mathematics called Graph
Theory has tools which aid in making an effective decomposition. A
short discussion will illustrate the potential utility of these techniques
and give an indication of the amount of work involved in reaping the
benefits. Such techniques are very important to developers of large-
scale simulation systems.

Given a flow network, as in Figure 5.2, where the rectangles
represent pieces of equipment (nodes) and the lines represent streams
(edges) joining the nodes, it is desired to represent the material flow,
in a general way, and then use this representation to help decompose
the system. To begin with, define an array called the Incidence Matrix [11], R. For a system of n nodes it will consist of n rows, corresponding to the sources of flow, and n columns, corresponding to
the destinations of flow. Thus, if the array consists of elements a_{ij},
the representation for flow going from node 1 to node 3 will be $a_{13} = 1$.

All elements a_{ij} for which there is no flow from node i to node j
will be zero. The incidence matrix for Figure 5.2 is

$$R = \begin{bmatrix} 0 & 1 & 0 & 0 \\ 0 & 0 & 1 & 0 \\ 0 & 1 & 0 & 1 \\ 0 & 0 & 0 & 0 \end{bmatrix}$$

(5.18)

R is sometimes referred to as the relation matrix. In order to obtain
useful information about the flow in the system being studied, some
simple techniques from Boolean algebra must be presented.

Note that the flow from node to node can represent material flow,
energy flow, or information flow. The latter case will be of special
interest for the solution of systems of equations. Such graphs showing the direction of flow are called directed graphs or digraphs.

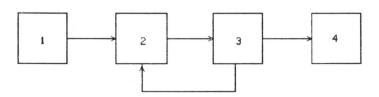

Figure 5.2 Simple flow network.

The edges are connective elements corresponding to such things as pipes, wires, or equations, in hydraulic, electrical, and equational systems, respectively. Further note that this analysis is associated with lumped systems (as opposed to distributed parameter systems).

5.5.1 Boolean Arithmetic

To find if there is a path n steps long in any network, compute R^n, using Boolean arithmetic. Any occurrence of a non-zero element indicates such a path.

Boolean Addition

Examples:

$$x + y = max(x,y)$$
$$1 + 0 = 1$$
$$1 + 1 = 1$$

Boolean addition is equivalent to the OR gate in logic circuits.

Boolean Multiplication

Examples:

$$x \cdot y = min(x,y)$$
$$1 \cdot 0 = 0$$
$$1 \cdot 1 = 1$$

Boolean multiplication is equivalent to the AND gate in logic circuits. With only these two operations the product of two vectors can be computed

$$(0 \quad 1 \quad 1 \quad 1 \quad 0) \begin{bmatrix} 1 \\ 1 \\ 0 \\ 1 \\ 1 \end{bmatrix} = 0 + 1 + 0 + 1 + 0 = 1$$

and hence the powers of R. Using the matrix of Equation 5.18 corresponding to the system in Figure 5.2, the powers of R can be computed as:

$$R^2 = \begin{bmatrix} 0 & 0 & 1 & 0 \\ 0 & 1 & 0 & 1 \\ 0 & 0 & 1 & 0 \\ 0 & 0 & 0 & 0 \end{bmatrix} \qquad (5.19)$$

The array 5.19 can be interpreted as indicating two step paths between the following nodes:

    1 to 3

    2 to 2

    2 to 4

    3 to 3

By also looking at Figure 5.2, it can be determined that the actual paths corresponding to the node list above are:

    1 to 2 to 3

    2 to 3 to 2

    2 to 3 to 4

    3 to 2 to 3

R^3 will indicate all of the paths of three steps.

$$R^3 = \begin{bmatrix} 0 & 1 & 0 & 1 \\ 0 & 0 & 1 & 0 \\ 0 & 1 & 0 & 1 \\ 0 & 0 & 0 & 0 \end{bmatrix} \qquad (5.20)$$

The terminating nodes for paths of length three are:

    1 to 2

    1 to 4

    2 to 3

    3 to 2

    3 to 4

Using R, R^2, and R^3, all of the nodes in the three step paths can be determined.

5.5.2 Reachability Matrix

By summing $R + R^2 + \ldots + R^k$, a matrix is obtained which represents all paths of k or less steps. As n, in equation 5.21, takes on higher values, a matrix is obtained which does not change as k increases. Such a representation is referred to as the reachability matrix, $R*$.

$$R* = \sum_{n=1}^{k} R^n \qquad (5.21)$$

The upper limit for k is the number of nodes in the network. But most systems will not have all nodes in one closed loop or reachable form all other nodes, so k will usually be less than that.

For the network in Figure 5.2, the reachability matrix is:

$$R^* = \begin{bmatrix} 0 & 1 & 1 & 1 \\ 0 & 1 & 1 & 1 \\ 0 & 1 & 1 & 1 \\ 0 & 0 & 0 & 0 \end{bmatrix} \qquad (5.22)$$

5.5.3 Loop Detection

If determining which nodes are members of a closed loop is of interest, the following matrix is formed:

$$RL = R* \cap [R^*]^T \qquad (5.23)$$

The loop matrix, RL, is the junction of $R*$ and its transpose. For Figure 5.2 it is:

$$RL = \begin{bmatrix} 0 & 0 & 0 & 0 \\ 0 & 1 & 1 & 0 \\ 0 & 1 & 1 & 0 \\ 0 & 0 & 0 & 0 \end{bmatrix} \qquad (5.24)$$

which can be interpreted as showing that node 2 is in a loop with node 3.

5.5.4 Network Decomposition [15,16]

Given the flow network in Figure 5.3, it is desired to find the flow rate in each stream. One approach is to write the node equations and other relationships to get n equations in n unknowns.

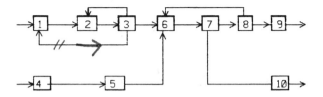

Figure 5.3 Decomposition network.

This would result in 10 node equations and four splitting equations
for nodes 3, 7, and 8.

Node	Equation ?
1	$y_1 = y_{12} + y_{13}$
2	$y_{12} + y_{32} = y_{23}$
3	$y_{23} = y_{36} + y_{32} + y_{31}$
4	$y_4 = y_{45}$
5	$y_{45} = y_{56}$
6	$y_{36} + y_{56} + y_{86} = y_{67}$
7	$y_{67} = y_{78} + y_{710}$
8	$y_{78} = y_{86} + y_{89}$
9	$y_{89} = y_9$
10	$y_{710} = y_{10}$

Splitting Equations[a]

$y_{31} = c1\, y_{32}$
$y_{36} = c2\, y_{32}$
$y_{78} = c3\, y_{67}$
$y_{89} = c4\, y_{78}$

[a]Where c1–c4 are
splitting factors.

Instead of solving all 14 equations simultaneously, it is obvious by inspection that some simplifications can be made, such as eliminating y_{45} or y_{56}. There is a formal procedure which indicates the order in which to solve the equations. The result of the procedure is a precedence table. Its construction is accomplished in the following fashion.

  1. Form R, the incidence matrix for the network for nodes. For Figure 5.3, it is

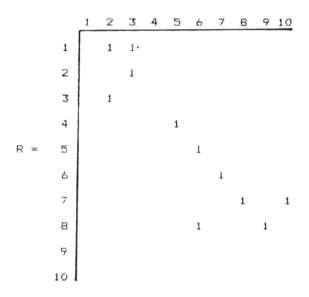

  2. Put all nodes with no precursors (ancestors) first. These correspond to nodes with all zeros in a column.

Precedence table

  1

  4

---

  3. Eliminate the rows and columns for nodes with no precursors.
  4. Put all nodes with no descendants last. These correspond to nodes with all zeros in a row.
  5. Eliminate the rows and columns for nodes with no descendants.
  6. Repeat Steps 2 through 5 until no further reduction is possible.

Precedence table

1

4

$\left.\begin{array}{c} \cdot \\ \cdot \\ \cdot \end{array}\right\}$ undetermined as yet

9

10

For the present example, the reduced incidence matrix is now:

$$R = \begin{array}{c|ccccc} & 2 & 3 & 6 & 7 & 8 \\ \hline 2 & & 1 & & & \\ 3 & 1 & & & & \\ 6 & & & & 1 & \\ 7 & & & & & 1 \\ 8 & & 1 & & & \end{array}$$

and the precedence table is:

Precedence table

1

4

5

$\left.\begin{array}{c} \cdot \\ \cdot \\ \cdot \end{array}\right\}$ undetermined as yet

9

10

---

7. Find all maximal cyclical networks (nets).
     A. A subgraph H containing n nodes of another graph G is defined as a cyclical net of order n if and only if (iff) each node of H is connected to every other node of H by a closed path.

B. A cyclical net H of order n in a graph G is said to be maximal in G iff every cyclical net in G is either a subgraph of H or contains no points in common with H. For example, in Figure 5.3, nodes 2 and 3 form a cyclical net, but not a maximal cyclical net.

If the matrix representing loops, RL, is formed for the present example, it will graphically show the maximal cyclical nets for this simple network. Using the reduced matrix from Step 6.

$$
RL = \begin{array}{c c}
 & \begin{array}{c c c c c} 2 & 3 & 6 & 7 & 8 \end{array} \\
\begin{array}{c} 2 \\ 3 \\ 6 \\ 7 \\ 8 \end{array} & \left|\begin{array}{c c c c c}
1 & 1 & & & \\
1 & 1 & & & \\
 & & 1 & 1 & 1 \\
 & & 1 & 1 & 1 \\
 & & 1 & 1 & 1 \\
\end{array}\right.
\end{array}
$$

Hence, the final entries in the precedence table.

Precedence table

1

4

5

2, 3

6, 7, 8

9

10

The precedence table can be interpreted as indicating that the equations corresponding to nodes 1, 4, and 5 should be solved successively in the order given. Next, a pair of simultaneous equations relating to nodes 2 and 3 should be solved, followed by the simultaneous solution of equations for nodes 6, 7, and 8. Finally, nodes 9 and 10 should yield simple equations to solve.

Consider now the possibility of taking advantage of structure in systems of equations. Take the problem of solving n equations in n unknowns. The number of operations required to solve such a set of equations can be proportional to n^3 as it is for a set of linear equations. If the equations are sparse, i.e., the number of variables appearing in any equation is considerably less than the total number of variables, it would be desirable to take advantage of this fact to aid in the solution.

Earlier in this section it was pointed out that for directed graphs, digraphs, it is possible to establish a precedence table indicating a preferred order of computation for recycle loops. For a system of equations, there is no *a priori* indication of direction of flow to help establish a digraph. But it might nevertheless be possible to do so if the information flow from one equation to another can be established. Take the following system of equations:

$$F1(x_1, x_2) = 0 \qquad\qquad (5.25)$$
$$F2(x_2) = 0$$
$$F3(x_1, x_3) = 0$$

This system of equations could be represented in an incidence matrix, I, as follows:

$$
\begin{array}{c}
\text{Variable} \\
\begin{array}{ccc}
1 & 2 & 3
\end{array}
\end{array}
$$

	1	2	3
Equation			
1	1	1	0
I = 2	0	1	0
3	1	0	1

Note that the system could be solved by finding x_2 from the second function, F2, then finding x_1 from the first function, F1, and finally by finding x_3 from the third function, F3.

In a sense, the process could be described as information flowing from equation 2 to equation 1 via variable x_2 and, similarly, information flowing from equation 1 to equation 3 via variable x_1. In system nomenclature, the output variable from one equation becomes the input variable to another. If variables can be chosen such that a unique variable appears in each pair of equations, then such a set of variables is called an output set. If the system of equations has a solution, there must exist an admissible output set. An admissible output set is one in which each and every row contains one and only one output variable and each column contains one and only one output variable.

By putting a pair of parenthesis around the diagonal elements in the incidence matrix, I, above, an admissible output set is indicated.

Thus, if every diagonal term in an incidence matrix is nonzero, one admissible output set will be obvious. However, it is not a requirement to have the diagonal terms be nonzero since the equations and the corresponding incidence matrix can be rearranged as

$$
\begin{array}{l}
F2(x_2) \\
F3(x_1,x_3), \ I = \\
F1(x_1,x_2)
\end{array}
\begin{bmatrix}
0 & (1) & 0 \\
1 & 0 & (1) \\
(1) & 1 & 0
\end{bmatrix}
$$

and the same output set is admissible. For this simple example, the admissible output set is unique, but in general that is not necessarily true.

Once an admissible output set has been obtained, methods similar to those shown earlier can be used to determine a precedence table [12].

Such techniques are great aids in solving large sets of equations. It is much easier, for example, to solve two sets of three simultaneous equations than to solve one set of six equations. The art in this whole process comes in balancing the effort spent on analyzing structure against the extra effort that might have been spent by brute-forcing the solution without regard to structure. For systems of several hundred equations in which only 10 or so variables appear in any one equation, great savings in computation time can be had by taking advantage of the structure.

5.6 STOCHASTIC SYSTEMS

All simulations are done with the intention of forecasting the behavior of the system under study. Such forecasting is to be considered much as weather forecasting. It does not predict the future with absolute certainty like a witch with a crystal ball, but rather indicates what the range of possibilities are and what, on the average, might be expected based on one's current knowledge of the system (all of which must be embedded within the simulation to have any effect).

Many books on operations research and Monte Carlo techniques contain abundant, detailed, and useful information about the simulation of essentially probabilistic systems [9]. The key features include representation of random distributions and a sophisticated record-keeping system to keep track of customer and service entities taking into consideration all of their featured characteristics and interactions. The enormity of the record-keeping task and why it is usually relegated to computers will become clear with the reading of Example 5.3 at the end of this section. The remainder of this section is intended as an overview of how stochastic simulation is undertaken and why it is so useful.

The stochastic problems for which modeling techniques are fairly well in hand can be categorized in several ways, but one useful approach is to clump them around the following areas.

1. Allocation: facilities available without interruption

2. Inventory: holding or storing a resource

3. Replacement: worn out or obsolete

4. Queuing: rule for selecting next entity to be processed

5. Sequencing and coordination: order in which things should be done

6. Routing: multiple entities/multiple destinations

7. Competition: external uncontrolled; risk involved; (zero sum markets)

8. Search: how much and what information; how to acquire and treat it.

The first four of these will be discussed in some detail. The last four are mentioned here only for completeness of presentation.

5.6.1 Allocation

A typical allocation problem can be stated as follows.

There are R_i amounts of resource i available and D_j demands for resource i. It costs c_{ij} to assign resource R_i to demand D_j.

The question then is how best to distribute the resources among the demands. Some measure of best must be established, such as minimum

$$\sum_i \sum_j c_{ij}$$

The demands might be represented as some probabilistic distribution and analysis made for successive times. The problem reduces to one modeled by linear or nonlinear programming depending on the formulation of constraints and objective function. Both of these areas are treated abundantly [2,3,7] and are outside the scope intended here.

5.6.2 Inventory

The classical inventory problem is one of determining how much of idle but useable resources to store and when and how much to order more of the resources. The variables involved are: (1) how much of a

certain resource to acquire, (2) when or how often to acquire the resource, and (3) the degree of completion of the stocked items. The
resources involved might be raw materials, parts of machines, complete machines, money, or even people with a certain skill. That
means that acquiring the resource could entail purchasing, producing, or recruiting, any one of which will have associated with it a
somewhat random time lag.

Most of the theoretical work published to date deals almost ex-
clusively with the determination of optimal operating doctrines for inventory systems consisting of a single stocking point and a single
source of supply. According to Hadley and Whitin [10], this is because: (1) many practical problems fall into this category, (2) the
mathematics is interesting even for this restricted case, and (3) it
is extremely difficult to determine optimal operating doctrines for more
complex systems.

The basic problem with inventory systems is that demands for
stocked entities can seldom be predicted with certainty. In addition,
for realistic systems, the acquisition times are also probabilistic in
nature.

A typical simple problem would be to consider an inventory situation in which resource entities are demanded one at a time, the number of entities demanded in a time period of specified length having
a probabilistic distribution (such as a Poisson distribution), with mean
demand rate being known or assumed. If the acquisition lead time is
known, the problem would be to determine the value I of the inventory
on hand which will trigger an order such that the probability of running out of stock and receiving one or more demands while the system
is out of stock is less than some small fraction.

Such problems assume that there are penalties for receiving demands which cannot be filled in the regular amount of time. The penalties might be directly monetary, as in late charges, or it might be
more severe, such as permanent loss of a client.

The inventory models can become rather complex by considering
even a small subset of significant parameters and variables involved,
such as reorder points, backorders, lead times, quantity discounts,
stockout costs, data acquisition and reliability, demand prediction,
determination of costs, procedural problems, measures and evaluations
of performance, and multi-echelon interactions.

5.6.3 Replacement

There are several areas related to replacement which are of a stochastic nature. These include replacement before or after failure, pre-
ventative maintenance, and reliability. Whether a piece of equipment
is replaced before or after failure depends upon the cost of replacement, the time to make the replacement, safety considerations, the

possibility of lost or substandard product, and obsolescence factors. Reliability is a subject which every design engineer should be concerned with. During the design phase the opportunity exists to estimate the useful life of a system. If the estimated life is too short, it can possibly be increased through the use of higher-quality parts or the addition of redundant subsystems. A good example of using the concept of reliability of systems is the design and manufacture of refrigerators. The self-lubricating motor and compressor systems for refrigerators designed a few decades ago were so reliable that it was common for these moving parts to last 20 or 30 years with no attention. With the advent of the concept of consumerism into the market place, the motor-compression systems for refrigerators were redesigned by some manufacturers so that the mean time to failure was closer to five years. This resulted in the use of cheaper parts and a higher turnover rate for the manufacturers engaged in this redesign. But, eventually, it also resulted in a disgruntled clientele and a rapid drop-off in sales to the point of going out of business.

As a case operating in the other direction, razor blades were, up until the 1950s only suitable for two or three shaves before they had to be discarded for being too dull. An enterprising manufacturer introduced a higher-quality and longer-lasting blade which increased the useful life to about one month. Even though the new blades cost more per blade, they cost much less per shave and the entire industry switched to making and marketing the higher-quality, longer-lasting blades.

In the case of equipment that wears out or becomes progressively more expensive to maintain, such as an automobile, there is a trade-off over an extended period of time between increased operating costs and periodic replacement. For example, one might consider a situation as shown below.

Trade-Off Costs for Automobile Replacement

Case	0	1	2	3	4	5	6	7	8	9	10
						Year					
A	9000	2500	2700	2800	2900	3400	3700	4000	4300	4700	5200
									TOTAL:		45,200
B	9000	2500	2700	2800	2900	9200	2600	2700	2800	2900	3400
									TOTAL:		43,500

The classic trade-off between increased maintenance costs in case A versus a new replacement, in year five for case B, illustrates the basic problem. But it is really more severe than the example presents because the costs involved are not known ahead of time. The problem then becomes stochastic in nature with some probabilities associated with incurring higher operating expenses as the years go by. Who knows when the transmission will go out requiring a major expense, or the air conditioner, etc.

Estimating reliability is an activity an engineer can make good use of during the design phase. The two most common ways of increasing reliability of a system are by: (1) upgrading the quality of a critical subassembly, and (2) adding functionally identical parts in parallel so that there is some redundancy to rely on if part of the system fails.

If there are n parallel parts where part i has a probability of failure of $p(i)$, then the probability that at least one of the parallel parts is working is

$$p(work) = 1 - [(1 - p1)(1 - p2) \ . \ . \ . \ (1 - pn)]$$

If there are m serial parts, where part j has a probability of $p(j)$ of functioning correctly, then the probability of the entire set working is

$$p(work) = p1 \cdot p2 \cdot \ . \ . \ . \ \cdot pm$$

At one point in the history of the design of computers the number of components was so large and the probability of working for each part so small that the computed probability of the computer functioning correctly was near zero. Fortunately, the development of solid-state devices as substitutes for vacuum tubes increased the reliability of the parts and the total system dramatically while at the same time reducing manufacturing costs and operating power consumption.

5.6.4 Queuing

A queue is a waiting line. Usually, it is a line of potential customers or clients waiting to be serviced at some facility, but it might be a queue of service facilities waiting to service a customer such as a taxi stand at a large hotel. Everyday life is full of queues at: post offices; banks; filling stations; ticket counters for movies; bus depots or airports; and grocery stores where there might be queues at the meat counter, at the pharmacy counter, at the checkout counter, or at the manager's office, to name a few. These can be single points of service, as at the theatre window, or multiple service points, as at the checkout counters in a supermarket. Sometimes the service at each

service point in a facility with multiple points is the same, as the grocery checkout, but there can also be multiple service points, some of
which provide different services, as filling station pumps that provide
different grades of gasoline.

All of these queues have in common the problem of determining
the order in which the facility services the customer. In many instances it is first in-first out (sometimes referred to as FIFO), while
at others, such as elevators, it is last in-first out (LIFO), and at still
others the priorities are set by some characteristic such as age, size,
or degree of emergency.

Formally, a queuing problem is said to exist if two conditions are
met: (1) either the arrival rate of the customers or the amount of
service facilities is subject to control, and (2) there are some kinds
of measurable costs associated with both the waiting time of the customers and the idle time of the facilities. The costs associated with
waiting customers is usually indirect. If a line is too long or moving
too slowly a decision might be made to go somewhere else for service.
This might result in a permanent transfer of business. But whether
a permanent or a one-time occurrence, the cost of lost business is
difficult to assess. The direct costs associated with idle facilities are
usually readily calculated.

The difficulties in most queuing problems are associated with
determining arrival time distributions, not in computing costs. The
random and widely varying distributions can usually only be estimated
assuming fundamental driving forces remain relatively stable. For example, airlines can estimate the average number of passengers on a
given route for a given day based on their historical records, but
when one of their planes crashes, or a sudden recession hits, their
normal estimates of customer loading are of limited value.

Example 5.3

Relatively simple cases of random arrival times can be treated mathematically if the probability of the next arrival's occurrence is independent of the time elapsed since the last arrival. Such a random distribution is called a Poisson distribution. In mathematically concise
notation, if Δt is a sufficiently small increment of time and r is the
average arrival rate (r = 1/average time between arrivals), the probability of an arrival in the interval t to t + Δt is equal to $r\Delta t$ and is
independent of t. The probability of n arrivals in any finite interval
of time is

$$p(rt) = \frac{e^{-rt}(rt)^n}{n!} \tag{5.26}$$

Equation 5.26 is called a Poisson distribution with parameter rt. It has a mean of rt and a variance of rt.

There are two circumstances in which the assumption of a Poisson distribution is likely to give poor results:

1. When arrivals are scheduled and the variance between actual and scheduled arrival times is small compared to the inter-arrival times.

2. When arrivals are time-dependent such as in the maintenance of fleet vehicles. Immediately after overhauls, the likelihood of maintenance is less than at other times and this violates one of the assumptions upon which the distribution is based.

If pn is the steady-state probability that there are n entities in the system, either being serviced or in a queue, ri is the Poisson arrival rate, and sn is the average service capacity per unit of time, then

$$pn = r0 \ r1 \ . \ . \ . \ rn - 1 \qquad\qquad (5.27)$$

and since there is some specific number of entities present in the system

$$p0 + p1 + \ . \ . \ . \ + pn + \ . \ . \ . \ = 1$$

Let

$$I = \frac{r}{s}$$

where I is referred to as the traffic intensity, then the average number of entities in the system is

$$
\begin{aligned}
N_{avg} &= p1 + 2p2 + 3p3 + \ . \ . \ . \\
&= (1 - p)[1 + 2I + 3I + \ . \ . \ . \ ]
\end{aligned}
$$

Recall from algebra that

$$1 + 2x + 3x + \ . \ . \ . \ = \frac{1}{(1 - x)^2}$$

from which it follows that

$$N_{avg} = \frac{I}{1 - I}$$

$$Q_{avg} = \frac{I^2}{1 - I}$$

where Q_{avg} is the average number in the queue in system and

$$S_{avg} = I$$

where S_{avg} is the average number being serviced in system. Note that

$$N_{avg} = S_{avg} + Q_{avg}$$

All this is to show how some of the parameters in a queuing system are developed. It was possible to make the calculations because of the simplifying assumptions about Poisson arrival times, exponential service times, etc.

Real systems usually do not fall into a straightforward category in which one tractable distribution is sufficient. They frequently have a mixture of scheduled arrivals and random arrivals with unequal probabilities of arrivals and service times. Consequently, simulation techniques are the only reasonable resort. Such languages as GPSS and GASP mentioned in Chapter 1 permit the use of mixed distributions. One system might have some queues with arrival times uniformly distributed and others normally or Poisson distributed. These simulation systems provide a reasonable vehicle for queuing phenomena as well as cases with various arrival and service characteristics, neither of which are handled by analytical methods.

Example 5.4: Bank Lobby

The basic features of a queuing process are presented in Figure 5.4 which depicts what might happen at a bank which has one queue for all windows. The triangles represent decision points.

Assume the bank service is as follows:

Three service windows

Average time to service one customer: 7 minutes

Service times are normally distributed with a standard deviation of 2 minutes

The lobby is only open from 9:30 a.m. until 12:30 p.m.

Customers arrive at the rate of one per minute

If the queue has 10 or more people, there is an even chance that an entering customer leaves before queuing.

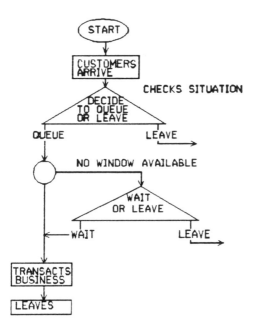

Figure 5.4 Bank queue.

If the queue has 15 or more people, the probability of leaving
is 0.9.

If a customer spends 30 minutes in the queue and is still not
about to be serviced, the probability of his leaving is 0.75.

On the average, how many customers leave without receiving service?
    Assume, for simplicity's sake, that the minimum time interval of
interest is one minute. If it is also assumed that the arrival rate distribution is Poisson with a parameter of 1, then the probabilities of
0, 1, 2, 3, and 4 arrivals per time period are .37, .37, .19, .06, and
.01.
    A uniform random number generator can be used to distribute
numbers between 0 and 100. Then, any number between 0 and 37
will represent no arrival, between 38 and 74 will be for 1 arrival,
73–93 for 2 arrivals, 94–99 for 3 arrivals, and 100 will represent
4 arrivals in a time period.
    Similarly, a random number uniformly distributed between 0 and
100 can represent service times. Since the service times are assumed
to be normally distributed, for convenience let the band about the
mean plus a half σ be 0.38 of the total, the next $\sigma = .24$, then 0.06,
then 0.01 as indicated in Table 5.2.

Table 5.2 Distribution of Service Times

Time to service	Fraction of distribution	Random number to represent
1	.01	1
2		
3	.06	2—4
4		5—7
5	.24	8—19
6		20—31
7	.38	32—69
8	.24	70—81
9		82—93
10	.06	94—96
11		97—99
12	.01	100

The distribution for whether a customer enters an existing queue, depending upon how long it is, can also be represented by random numbers from 1 to 100.

If number in queue < 10   p(enter queue) = 1

                = 11—14   = 0.5 (1—50 enters)
                                                (51—100 leaves)
                > 15
                                          = 0.1 (1—10 enters)
                                                (11—100 leaves)

Table 5.3 gives the details of the simulation of the first 21 minutes of the business day. The column headed "Cust. I.D." indicates the label for each arriving customer. The simulation process entails starting at time increment 9:30, getting a random number for the arrival distribution, in this case 40, which translates from the distribution assignments given earlier into one arrival during this time period. Each arrival is assigned an identification number for purposes of keeping track of the customers. These are assigned sequentially so the I.D. number also serves as a counter of how many customers have entered the system.

The number of arrivals in each time interval can be assigned one after the other by generating a sequence of random numbers and using them to determine whether there are 0, 1, 2, 3, or 4 arrivals during a given period. The sequence of random numbers that was generated for determining arrivals is given in the second column headed "Arr. rnd." In the adjacent column are the number of arrivals in the period corresponding to the random number distribution given earlier.

Table 5.3 Details of Bank Lobby Simulation

Time	Arr. rnd.	Lobby ar	Lobby dp	In queue	Window 1 ar	Window 1 dp	Window 2 ar	Window 2 dp	Window 3 ar	Window 3 dp	Cust. I.D.	Ser. rnd.	Ser. time (min)	Stay rnd.
9:30	40	1			1						1	59	7	
9:31	46	1					2				2	37	7	
9:32	48	1							3		3	26	6	
9:33	26	0									0			
9:34	37	0									0			
9:35	60	1		1							4	18	5	
9:36	58	1		2							5	79	8	
9:37	86	2	1	3		1					6, 7	15 38	5 7	
9:38	13	0	2	1	4			2		3	0			
9:39	83	2		3			5		6		8, 9	89, 2	9, 3	
9:40	35	0		3							0			
9:41	44	1		4							10	79	8	
9:42	74	1		5							11	73	8	
9:43	63	1	1	5		4					12	53	7	
9:44	73	1	1	5	7					6	13	5	4	
9:45	46	1		6					8		14	40	7	

Table 5.3 (Continued)

Time	Arr. rnd.	Lobby ar	Lobby dp	In queue	Window 1 ar	Window 1 dp	Window 2 ar	Window 2 dp	Window 3 ar	Window 3 dp	Cust. I.D.	Ser. rnd.	Ser. time (min)	Stay rnd.
9:46	49	1		7							15	60	7	
9:47	76	2	1	8				5			16, 17	34 / 98	7 / 11	
9:48	59	1		9			9				18	77	8	
9:49	80	2		11							19, 20	71 / 48	8 / 7	
9:50	80	2		13							21, 22	9, 60	5, 7	
9:51	5	0	2	11		7		9			0			

[a]Arr. rnd. = arrival random number, Cust. I.D. = customer identification number, Ser. rnd. = service random number, Ser. time = service time (based on Ser. rnd.), Stay rnd. = stay in queue, ar = arrival, dp = departure.

Table 5.4 Customer Summary

Customer number	Arrival time	Departure time	Queue time	Service time	Total time
1	9:30	9:37	0	7 min	7 min
2	9:31	9:38	0	7	7
3	9:32	9:38	0	6	6
4	9:35	9:43	3	5	8
5	9:36	9:47	3	8	11
6	9:37	9:44	2	5	7
7	9:37	9:51	7	7	14
8	9:39	9:53	6	9	15
9	9:39	9:51	9	3	12
10	9:41	—	—	—	—

Associated with each arrival is a column of random numbers, headed "Ser. rnd.," which is used to determine the service time for each customer. Given the "Ser. rnd.," the actual service time is taken from Table 5.2. Thus, customer 8 has a "Ser. rnd." of 89 and, from Table 5.2, that corresponds to a service time of 9 minutes. Of course, the service time is not applied until the customer reaches a service window. Customer 8 arrived at the bank at 9:39, but had to wait in the queue until 9:45 and then had a service time of 9 minutes, departing the window at 9:54 (not shown).

For a complete simulation of the bank lobby, there would be 181 time increments to cover the time from 9:30 until 12:30. Even though the entire simulation is not shown, Table 4.3 shows enough details of how the simulation could be conducted while Tables 5.4 and 5.5 and Figure 5.5 present some of the kinds of data which are immediately available from such simulations.

Figure 5.5 is somewhat misleading because the simulation was not carried out for long enough time to reflect the true distribution of waiting times. From the early minutes, the number in the queue starts

Table 5.5 Facilities Use Summary

Window	Idle time	Busy time	Total time	Percent idle
1	0	22	22	0
2	1	21	22	4.5
3	2	20	22	9.1

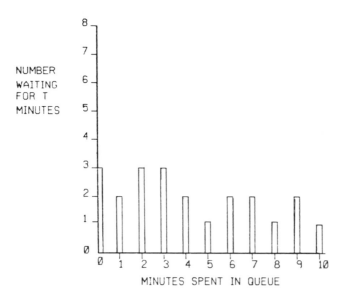

Figure 5.5 Distribution of times in queue.

growing and continues to grow. The option of people leaving after waiting 15 or 20 minutes did not take effect yet either. But Figure 5.5 graphically illustrates some of the information that can be developed through simulation.

This simple example vividly portrays how much information is contained in even a very simple simulation of a stochastic queuing system. It also shows clearly that intuition is not of much value in estimating critical parameters. If other realistic considerations, such as special service windows, opening additional windows or closing some of the windows, different service times for experienced tellers as compared to new tellers, and different arrival times depending on the time of day (such as lunch periods and the time just after most offices close), were included in the problem, it would be hopeless to solve the problem with any means other than a computer simulation. As it is, any of the complicating factors mentioned could easily be accommodated in a simulation, especially if it were done on a computer using one of the sophisticated simulation languages.

REFERENCES

1.   Hadley, G., *Linear Programming*, Addison-Wesley, Reading, Massachusetts, 1962.

2. McMillan, C., *Mathematical Programming*, 2nd ed., Wiley, New York, 1970.

3. Beveridge, G. and R. Schechter, *Optimization: Theory and Practice*, McGraw-Hill, New York, 1970.

4. Dorn, W., and D. McCracken, *Numerical Methods with Fortran IV Case Studies*, Wiley, New York, 1972.

5. Von Rosenberg, D., *Methods for the Numerical Solution of Partial Differential Equations*, American Elsevier, New York, 1969.

6. Faddeeva, V. N., *Computational Methods of Linear Algebra*, Dover, New York, 1959.

7. Himmelblau, D. M., *Applied Nonlinear Programming*, McGraw-Hill, New York, 1972.

8. Dennis, J. E., and J. J. More, "Quasi-Newton Methods, Motivation and Theory," *SIAM Rev.*, *19*(1):46–89 (1977).

9. Ackoff, R. L. and M. W. Sasieni, *Fundamentals of Operations Research*, Wiley, New York, 1968.

10. Hadley, G., and T. M. Whitin, *Analysis of Inventory Systems*, Prentice-Hall, Englewood Cliffs, New Jersey, 1963.

11. Himmelblau, D. M., and K. B. Bischoff, *Process Analysis and Simulation: Deterministic Systems*, Wiley, New York, 1968.

12. Steward, D. V., "On an Approach to Techniques for the Analysis of the Structure of Large Systems of Equations," *SIAM Rev.*, *4*(4):321–342 (1962).

13. Hamming, R. W., *Numerical Methods for Scientists and Engineers*, McGraw-Hill, New York, 1962.

14. Scarborough, J. B., *Numerical Mathematical Analysis*, Johns Hopkins U. Press, Baltimore, 1955.

15. Barkley, R. W., and R. L. Motard, "Decomposition of Nets," *Chem. Eng. J.*, *3*:265 (1972).

16. Upadhye, R. S., and E. A. Grens, "Selection of Decompositions for Process Simulation," *A.I.Ch.E. J.*, *21*:136 (1975).

17. Ingels, D. M., *Analysis of Flow in Pipeline Networks*, Masters Thesis, University of Oklahoma, 1962.

18. Anonymous, *Bulletin 286*, University of Illinois Engineering Station, Urbana, Illinois, 1936.

19. Ingels, D. M., and J. E. Powers, "Analysis of Pipeline Networks," *Chem. Eng. Prog.*, Feb. 1964, pp. 65–70.

20. Christenson, J. H., Personal communication.

6

DEVELOPING THE COMPUTER MODEL

The purpose of computers is to produce insight, not numbers.

[R. W. Hamming]

6.1 INTRODUCTION

Programming in specific languages for specific computers is described in multifarious books and manuals. Guidelines are presented here for efficient programming specifically relating to models for engineering applications.

A computer simulation is implemented ultimately as a series of computer programs. No matter how carefully all of the work leading up to the program is done, the program produces the final result by which the project is judged. It must be done correctly.

Conversely, no matter how brilliantly the program represents the model, if the model is deficient in some way or the objectives are inadequate, the first to receive blame will be the computer program. More insidiously, though, printed results are sanctified. Computer programs do exert influence.

6.2 STRUCTURED APPROACH

The methodology summarized in Chapter 2 indicated the wisdom of building models starting from the simple and working up to the

complex. A useful way to help accomplish this is to approach the programming effort in a modular fashion.

First, outline the overall algorithm by function or process. This
can start as a skeletal executive which merely calls the individual functions as required. Then create a separate set of subroutines for each
function or process. These separate modules can be tested individually.
When one tests out as good, then it can be added to the skeletal executive, which simply acts as a traffic director.

Different individuals can write various modules for a multiperson
team. Any considerations of common nomenclature can be rationalized
when the module is incorporated into the skeletal executive. However,
it is good planning and more efficient if some standards and procedures
for nomenclature and structure are issued before the development of
the modules begins.

When a separate module is developed, a temporary driver, functioning like the overall executive but calling only the minimum necessary modules to test the one at hand, should be written and documented for check-out purposes. Due to the iterative nature of software development, any module is subject to change. Therefore, the
individual testing executives will come in handy.

Figure 6.1 represents such a skeletal executive for simulating
Example 5.4. The boxes contain enough information to check the order
of computation and the logical flow of information, but not enough to
write the program from directly except as a series of subprogram calls
where each box in the skeletal executive represents a subprogram.
Initially, these subprograms can be dummies.

6.2.1 Algorithms

An algorithm is a process by which something is accomplished. It shows
what must be done and the order in which it must be done. The most
difficult part of any computer modeling or simulation development is to
develop a suitable algorithm. It is not enough to have a set of equations: the actual steps of allowing the values of the variables to be
set and solving the equations must be described.

For example, suppose the problem is described as: find the minimum value of the scalar $y(x)$ such that

$$x_1 + x_2 = 3$$
$$x_1, x_2, x_3 > 0$$
$$-5x_2 + x_3 < 17$$
$$y = 17x_1 + 2x_2 - x_3$$

The equations and inequalities are simple in form. It might be possible
to brute-force one's way to the solution of this particular set of

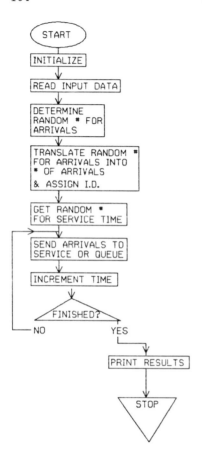

Figure 6.1 Skeletal executive for bank.

relationships, but it belongs to a class of problems in which the objective function, y(x), is linear, all of the constraint equations are linear, and the objective function is to be optimized, i.e., either a minimum or a maximum is to be found. The solution procedure for this class of problems is referred to as linear programming. Many general algorithms for solving this class of problems now exist [3]. But the point is, the solution procedure for this type of problem, especially if hundreds of variables are involved, is not straightforward if one happens not to be aware of the existing algorithms. Even for the simplest model, it is necessary to develop an efficient and logically complete algorithm.

A logically complete algorithm accounts for misinformation and incomplete information. Suppose the problem is to find the length of the radius of a circle of known area. The algorithm is simple, right?

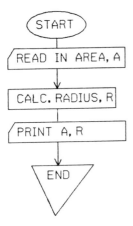

However, suppose someone inadvertently gave a negative value for the area, A. What will the computer do if it tries to take the square root of a negative number? Most likely, it will stop and if one is lucky, it will print an error message which will allow the programmer to determine why the program stopped. In fact, the algorithm is incomplete because it does not trap or intercept the faulty input.

A better result would have been achieved if the algorithm anticipated the problem of taking the square root of the negative number. The algorithm thus protects against the program stopping or at least pinpoints the cause exactly. It might be as below.

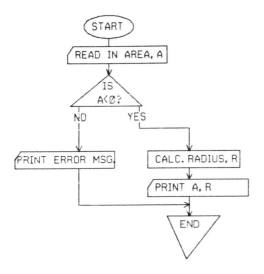

This simple example merely illustrates one point about anticipating difficulties by examining the input-data. Good algorithms always make provision for error trapping, as it is referred to, and printing out messages indicating the source of the error.

Drawing flow charts or flow diagrams allows one to check the algorithm for logical completeness and consistency. Most of the problems with software development occur not in expressing equations, but in the logic, i.e., developing the algorithm to cover all cases completely and consistently. The messy problems are in logic, not mathematical expressions.

The flow chart should not show too much computational detail, but rather stress the logical flow of information and the order in which things are done. All decision points should be indicated. At least two levels of detail are highly useful. The overall flow chart does not have much detail but shows the entire algorithm. Blocks from the overall flow chart can be expanded to show more detailed logic. This is all consistent with the modular approach in model development described in Chapter 4.

Developing complete algorithms is the hardest part of software development, but it also pays off with the greatest rewards. The flow charts should always come before one line of code has been written. They will be invaluable in program development, during debugging, for documentation, and later when the software is operational and some-one wants to study the logic of the algorithm to check its validity or add some enhancement to the program.

Example 6.1: Algorithm Development

Develop the algorithm to calculate the length of the hypotenuse of a right triangle given that the lengths of the sides forming the right angle are A and B.

Algorithm

1. Start

2. Read in A and B

3. Calculate hypotenuse = $\sqrt{A^2 + B^2}$

4. Write out A, B, and hypotenuse

To check for errors in the input oata, the algorithm might be expanded somewhat as indicated in the flow chart below.

The flow diagram in Figure 6.2 shows the logic developed for the computer model of the hydraulic network. This problem lends itself to being developed in several modules as follows:

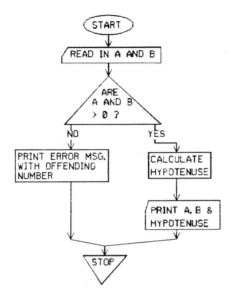

1. Executive routine

2. Input

3. Calculate friction factor

4. Calculate R, the correction factor

5. Output

The structured approach can thus be fruitfully applied without much struggle to decompose the problem into logical modules.

By default, with the structure given above, the executive routine would perform all calculations not associated with any of the other modules. This would include the loop pressure drop calculations, checking for convergence, etc.

The input routine should always be a separate logical entity. Initial versions of the input methods would include reading all data directly from the keyboard since this is easy to program. As the program is used more, it will become obvious that most of the data for a problem won't be changing from one run to the next. This leads naturally to storing the data on a diskette. From the disk, it can be read back in at any time and only those items which need to be changed will need to be inputed through the keyboard.

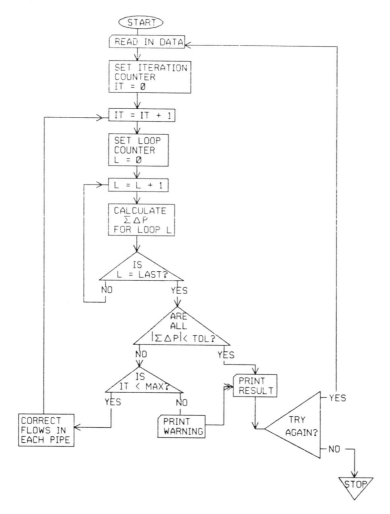

Figure 6.2 Algorithm for pipe network.

The friction factor subroutine can be written and validated for ranges of the relative roughness and Reynold's number as a separate job. Once it has been validated, it can easily be called by the executive routine of the hydraulic problem when necessary. The same is not quite true of the correction factor, R, required for the modified Hardy-Cross method. Here, the flow rates around a loop must be known and it is easier to check out these calculations with the code embedded in the total procedure as a subroutine. Logically, any of the several methods summarized in Olujic [6] could be used to calculate the friction factor, as long as the subroutine for calculating R were consistent with it.

The management of the output section is somewhat like that of the input section. Initially it will be simple, displaying only the minimum information to verify that the procedure is working. As experience with the system develops, demands for different formats, disk storage of system data, different units, etc., will grow. Keeping the output code as a coherent package allows the smooth transition from one version to the next as improvements and modifications in the output are made.

6.3 RESOURCE REQUIREMENTS

Computer models and simulation packages run the gamut from a few lines of code to several hundred thousand lines of code. There is a "chicken-egg" relationship associated with the size and speed of the computer hardware and the size of the software written for a particular machine. For instance, there are project management models, of the CPM/PERT genre, which can be run on personal computers such as the Apple, but programs in this same area are also available for large systems of IBM mainframes and, in fact, are such large programs that they require the virtual storage features some systems offer. The larger programs are suitable to help manage such mammoth projects as NASA's space shuttle effort or the development of an entire petrochemical complex by some integrated oil company. Obviously, an Apple computer would be inappropriate and insufficient to handle such large projects.

The point is, that the hardware/software can be chosen to match the needs of the project. If a company operates a computer center which has a large sophisticated program available, it probably would be good to use what is available even if it amounts to killing a fly with a sledge hammer. But if hardware/software are yet to be selected, there is a bewildering array of possibilities to choose from.

Table 6.1 presents a rough guide for the selection of hardware based on problem requirements.

Table 6.1 Rough Hardware Selection Guide

| | Suitable system | | |
Problem characteristic	Micro (P.C.)	Mini	Maxi
Number of variables	< 10	< 200	Any number
Number of eqns/in-equalities	< 10	< 200	Any number
Real time	20 data pts.	1000 pts.	Not used
Lines of software	< 5000	< 50,000	Any number
Number of interactive terminals	1 or 2	< 16	Dollar limit, not performance

The self-obvious statement can be made: use small resources to attack small problems. This is effective for two reasons: (1) smaller resources, like personal computers, are usually easier to gain access to (there are more of them around), and (2) smaller resources are easier to interface with. Because they are not as versatile, they require less knowledge to use. This is a great benefit to inexperienced users in particular.

Personal computers will continue to grow in both popularity and in computing power. More significant models and simulations will be performed on them. But if the applications become ambitious enough, one will still have to resort to larger mainframes.

Computer operating systems, from the user's viewpoint, operate in one of two modes: batch or interactive. In the batch mode, the complete input is offered, whereupon the computer, or some fraction of it, is dedicated to running the job to completion without any interruptions. There is no interplay between the user and the computer while the job is being processed. Input is usually via punched cards, magnetic tape, or from a disk file. Output is usually to a line printer, magnetic tape, or disk file. Typical turnaround time, the time between job submittal and receiving the result, varies from a few minutes to a few days depending on the job size and how busy the computer installation is.

In the interactive mode, as the term implies, there is, or can be, regular interaction between the user and the computer. This interaction requires a video display screen and a keyboard whether there is data transmitted via some other input media or not. Turnaround times are usually on the order of a few seconds to a few minutes. The benefits are that the human decisionmaking element remains an integral part of the process. This allows creative design and penetrating "what if" studies to be carried out in an efficient manner. It also frees up

the user from being a computer-programming expert. He only needs
to select appropriate entries from a series of menus.

6.3.1 Effect of Word Size

Word size affects basically two things: (1) how many digits the machine can handle automatically while doing arithmetic, and (2) how
many locations have unique addresses within core. Both of these aspects are somewhat transparent to users, but they do have some rami-
fications for modeling and simulation.

The number of digits used in the lowest-level arithmetic affects
the ultimate computational speed, especially where floating-point
arithmetic is concerned. The fewer bits in a word, the longer it
takes to perform arithmetic preserving, say, 10 digits of precision.
Computers with eight-bit processors, such as most early personal computers, thus suffer from relatively slow floating-point arithmetic computation. Since most simulations use floating-point arithmetic, they
are adversely affected by a small word size. A detailed discussion of
computer words and floating point arithmetic is contained in Bennett
and Evert [5].

The maximum address within core at any time is also limited by
the largest integer that a word can hold. Most eight-bit processors
use a "double word" and thus have 2^{16} or 65,536 (called 64k) address-
able locations, or bytes. Any program which can be contained within
that limitation can reside in core all at the same time. Programs larger than this must be carefully decomposed into segments which can
be called into core from secondary storage devices. Such chaining or
overlaying takes considerable time in shuffling segments into and out
of core which in turn slows execution down further.

As with any other craft, the developer must choose the right-
sized tool for the job intended. Relatively small models which don't
require a lot of iterative calculations can reasonably be done on personal computers, which until recently were part of a class of machines
referred to as microcomputers.

Computers have been classified as micros, minis, or mainframes
for the past several years. The classification was based primarily on
the number of bits in a machine word, being eight for micros, 16 for
minis, and 32 and above for main frames. However, the fundamental
building-block chips for personal computers have evolved from eight-
bit processors to 16-bit processors with 32-bit machines already in
prototype. That means that the old labels of micro, mini, and mainframe are no longer meaningful, the main distinction of word length
having been confounded.

Newer, more powerful, and smaller chips will continue to be developed so that the machines evolving from what were once called
microcomputers will have more features, compute faster, and hold more

numbers than most of the machines currently referred to as mainframes. Some characteristic(s) other than the number of bits per
word will have to be used to distinguish between classes of computers.

The implications for modeling and simulation are good. Personal
computers will grow ever faster, with larger core sizes, making more
jobs feasible and distributing the equipment so that machines will always be near at hand when a problem arises.

6.3.2 Input/Output

Input

There has been progressive development from fixed field, fixed format to variable field, free form data requirements, to user friendly,
menu driven input with interactive cueing and default values. With
early batch processing, all input had to be fixed and exactly anticipated. With interactive input today, logic can guide the program to
query the user for information when it is needed and only for those
things that are required. Default values are presented with override
capability. Judgements can then be made of partial results and
branches selected directly by the user for pursuing different processing based on his judgement.

Early programs required keypunching which resulted in punched
cards for input. It was a good time to own stock in paper companies.
Every error meant at least one card was thrown away. When a card
deck was dropped it was often a disaster.

Most input now is via CRTs which are more efficient and less
wasteful of resources. There are also refinements such as light pens,
digitizing tables, and interactive menu tablets. Ergonomics has bloomed
and improved the color, eyestrain, contrast, location of keyboard and
screen, resolution, etc., to further increase the productivity of the
basic input activity.

Data bases on disk and tape allow recalling data from previous
cases and only changing pertinent parameters. Data stored on electronic media require adequate backup. There are no decks to drop
and scramble, but a scratched disk surface from a crashed disk head
makes all data on that disk nonrecoverable.

Output

The form of computer output has evolved from just a collection of tiny
lights on the face of a computer control panel to line printers that can
print several thousand lines per minute and laser printers which can
produce multiple fonts, various orientations on the page, print on
both sides of a page, and do it all in color.

Output can still be on punched cards, magnetic tapes, hard
disks, floppy disks, line printers, plotters, and video screens.

Three-dimensional holography has been demonstrated in prototypes. The improvements and increases in media types continue, all for the benefit of the user.

There are some recurring problem areas with computer output, of which three are chief. First, many programs produce more output than any human being can reasonably digest. The thesis seems to be that if a little bit of data is good, a lot must be great. Unfortunately, this is not so. Five hundred pages of traced output is an unreasonable amount of information to wade through and a waste of paper.

The second recurring problem area is that computer output tends to become "sanctified." This phenomenon is an extension of "what ever is in print must be correct." A jaundiced eye must be cast over every computer output, especially on that emanating from a software package that has only recently been commissioned. However, even mature software can produce misleading results if poor quality data are fed into the program.

The third problem area, which has not been diminished with time and developments, has been alluded to earlier. It is the need for back up. Electronic media require back up of a different nature than paper records, an aspect discussed in more detail in Section 6.3.4.

In summary, there are basically two types of output: physical output, such as cards, printed pages, plots, punched tapes, and microfiches; and electronic output, such as magnetic tapes, disks, and video screens. Only printing on paper and video screen is readily readable by people and will continue to be the primary output media for human consumption.

Some simulation programs produce lots of output. This can best be digested if it is also presented in organized groups of related information. In other words, well-designed reports should be a normal function of a good simulation package.

6.3.3 Centricity

Early computer applications were rather small compared to today's. Input was predominantly via punched cards and output split between cards and line printers. There were no devices for permanently storing data files electronically. Necessarily, the job stream coming to the computer was the primary focus in the software area. This job stream usually consisted of a deck of cards representing the program, followed by the input data. Card file cabinets full of programs abounded. Some data decks, which tended not to change much from run to run, were also stored in the card files. The primary emphasis of every computer installation was the development, procurement, use, storage, and documentation of computer programs. It was a program-centric universe and rightly so.

As the computers systems evolved and more and more software became not only available, but mature, large files of data became increasingly important, leading to the rapid hardware development in media for electronic file storage such as ever larger and faster random access disks, magnetic tapes, and mass storage devices.

Corporations and data centers began to change their perspective about which was the more valuable resource; data or programs. Large data bases, whether they were corporate financial information such as budget and accounting data, or collections of technical information such as physical, chemical, or mechanical properties of a large number of materials, proliferated. These data bases grew over a period of several years, even decades, and were the source of input data for not one, but many different application programs. Such data bases are corporate resources which would be hard to replace or duplicate if lost.

The tendency now is to treat application areas in which data are ad hoc but the program large and stable as program centric, but to treat areas in which there are large data bases providing input to many programs as data centric. Computer installations usually have a propensity to be either one or the other.

Large-scale simulations can fall into either category. Sometimes the simulation model is relatively large and stable with the input data changing from run to run. In other instances, the input data are so numerous that they form a data base which is permanently maintained for simulations and other computer applications too. A well-designed simulation program will be able to accept its input by specifying only a file name, and will generate a file for output not only for the final result, but one from which restart and continuation of the simulation can be made.

There might be many cases to study and both the input data sets and their subsequent simulation output data sets would be stored as so many files which can be archived and accessed at any time. Each potential application must be evaluated as to the merits of data versus program centricity.

6.3.4 Security

Electronically stored information is subject to loss in ways that paper or microfiche are not. Since computer disks and tapes use magnetic phenomena to represent data, they are vulnerable to electric fields. Sources of problems are power surges in the supply circuit, static electricity, and lightening.

Disks and other on-line devices are most vulnerable. Magnetic tapes, stored in a cabinet, are the least vulnerable. At anytime during the processing of a job, a disk read or write head could fail, sometimes referred to as "crash," causing mechanical damage to the recording surface. When this occurs, all files on that disk are irretrievably lost.

The only protection against such a potential disaster is to provide data backup. Thus, periodically or on demand, all information on a disk is copied to another device, frequently a magnetic tape. Such redundancy uses up resources, but anyone who has suffered the loss of significant data that was not backed up will testify that this ounce of prevention is worth a pound of cure. (It just doesn't have the right ring to it to say "A gram of prevention is worth a kilo of cure.")

Making redundant copies of electronically stored data is a form of operational security. In this same area of security, there is the problem of controlling access to information. Who gets access to payroll information, to other personnel records, to corporate financial data, to proprietary technical data, long-range plans, etc., all of which might be stored in a computer file?

The most common security method used today is to require some form of identification and passwords, first of all to get access to the computer at all, and secondly to access specific files. Modeling and simulation activities don't normally suffer too much in this area, but they can involve the use of sensitive data during "what if" studies by corporate officers.

6.4 CHARACTERISTICS OF GOOD SOFTWARE

It can be said that the only criterion for good software that really counts is: it works! But just like the Wright brothers' airplane, although it worked, there was still room for some improvement. The characteristics for good software are discussed not only for modeling and simulation, but for programs in general. Some of the characteristics apply only to programs operating in a batch mode, and some only to those operating in an interactive mode, and will be identified as such. Finally, a much overlooked and underemphasized aspect, documentation, will be dealt with in some detail.

6.4.1 Structure

All good software is modular. It might be most efficient to operate and cover all possible cases, but if it is not modular, it will lead to serious problems. The kind of problems that accrue from monolithic software packages are: difficulties in updating, maintaining, modifying, and sometimes in making it transportable or translatable to other computers.

For batch process software, the gross structure should be developed around three parts:

Preprocessor

Main function

Postprocessor

The batch preprocessor has the function of checking the entire input file for possible errors. It should check to see if all required data are present and are within reasonable ranges, and give explicit and lucid error and warning messages for any suspected noncompliance. The entire file should be scanned, if possible. If any fatal errors are found, execution of the main function should not even be initiated.

The main function part of the software should itself be modular. Whether a program is written for batch or interactive mode it should have the following characteristics:

Efficient code

Error traps so the program is always in control

Technically correct results

Robustness

Extensive testing

Reasonable input requirements

Default values where possible

Appropriate output of reasonable detail and format

The batch mode postprocessor should allow various types of analysis and report generation from the results of the main function. Sometimes, special forms of output such as sketches or plots are produced as well as textual reports and numerical tables. For simulation programs which are run for multiple cases, the postprocessor might manipulate the output files to extract data from different cases for comparison or trend presentation.

Software written for the interactive mode has a considerably different structure from that written for the batch mode. Whereas the basic structure of the latter is linear, i.e., the preprocessor executes followed by the main function, followed by the post processor, the basic structure of interactive software is hierarchical or tree structured. This structure manifests itself to the user as a hierarchical set of menus which allow use of powerful software with no knowledge of computer programming. The user has only to select one option from each menu displayed on the screen to effect execution of the software in the desired fashion. Such an approach opens up the use of computers to an audience about an order of magnitude larger than if some, however basic, knowledge of programming were required.

6.4.2 Transportability

Transportability is a measure of the ability to take a program working on one type of computer and running it on another type. This is important if the program is to have the widest possible distribution, a desirable feature for whoever is marketing or maintaining a simulation package. For the agency maintaining a software package, the more compatible the versions are for various computers, the easier it is to maintain all at the same degree of updatedness. Within a company which is only a user, it would be of consequence if: (1) the company had several types of computers on which it wanted to run the program, (2) it had significant simulations already running on machine A but it was going to be replaced by machine B, a newer computer, or (3) such a large portion of the company's business was involved with the simulations that it didn't want to feel married to the vendor on whose machines it was currently implemented.

For any or all of the reasons above, transportability is usually considered desirable. The possible source languages affect, in a fundamental way, how transportable the programs might be. Assembly language, while the most powerful and versatile (for a given machine), is highly machine dependent. Any simulation program written in assembly language should be considered as being not transportable.

At the other end of the spectrum, programs written in ANSI Fortran or other standard Fortrans are essentially totally transportable; i.e., if a standard Fortran is implemented on machine A and B, then any Fortran program running on A will also run on B without any programming changes. Other languages fall somewhere between these two extremes, usually requiring reprogramming at least in the input/-output instructions. PL1, in particular, was developed by IBM and has been implemented at best halfheartedly by other manufacturers and is, thus, pretty well restricted to IBM computers (admittedly, a large population).

Some subtle differences in compilers and some not-so-subtle hardware differences, such as word length, can cause programs to behave differently on different computers. In particular, convergence tests are frequently of the form

is $\left| x_n - x_{n-1} \right|$ .LE. eta

where

x_n = The variable on iteration n

x_{n-1} = The variable on iteration n − 1

.LE. = Less than or equal

eta = Some small positive number which is the tolerence

Using identical input data for a simulation run on two different computers can give quite different results, especially if eta approaches the precision limit of a word. For example, if machine A has essentially 10 digits of precision while machine B has only seven, then, for a value of eta $= 1 \cdot 10^{-8}$, the program might converge on machine A but not converge on B.

Roundoff and truncation differences from one machine to another are notorious sources of seemingly incompatible results for identical problems running on identical code.

6.4.3 Input/Output

The current jargon describing the desired attributes for the interface between user and computer is "user friendly." For a software package to be truly user friendly it should have at least these five characteristics:

1. Interactive

2. Menu driven

3. Reasonable response time

4. Reasonable amount of input and output

5. User always knows what to do next

Having an interactive system involves the user in an active fashion. This approach permits the user to make decisions based on intermediate results and exercise his creativity and analytical talents, and is the primary reason why interactive computing is so heavily favored by computer users.

The menu approach is what basically frees the user from having to be a "computer jock." Practically anyone can pick a number from one to six and, in fact, four-year-old children are using computers to play games via menu-driven software.

In the interactive mode, desirable time delays for the computer to respond to a user input are around two seconds. A user won't feel totally abandoned if it takes up to 15 seconds, but if the computer sits there for much longer than that without indicating what it is doing, the time will exceed the user's attention span and the primary benefit of the interactive mode will be lost.

As an example, one disk backup program takes about five minutes to read, write, and verify that a good copy has been made of an entire disk. While it is processing, it displays a table of all the sectors and as each sector is read, written, and verified, it displays which activity it is performing in the space indicated for the given sector. The net result is that the user, while unable to do anything else on the computer, knows what the program is doing and approximately how far along in the job it is. It is a good process to use for executions taking over a quarter of a minute.

The characteristics of good input and output are that they be meaningful and place reasonable demands on the user. For the interactive mode, hand-entered input should be minimized with default values and permanent data files providing the bulk of the input. Because most video screens and the software which drives them are capable of graphical presentations, one's imagination and available programming time are the only limits to meaningful and attractive output for interactive systems, even to the point of producing animated presentations, something that cannot be done on hard copy media such as paper and transparencies. If a picture is worth 1000 words, what's a colored moving picture worth? By the same token, 500 pages of numbers is indigestable.

6.4.4 Programmer Friendliness

In addition to being user friendly, good software is programmer friendly. The main characteristics to achieve this are:

Well documented internally and externally

Logically laid out and written with flow charts

Statement labels in ascending order

Descriptive variable names

Modular

No cutesy tricks using eccentric features of hardware/software

Built-in debugging aids

The manager of the software development should expect that the person who writes the program will not be around to answer questions or modify it when it gets used in every conceivable way. While it is most important to get a program working, it is only good business to have the job finished so that someone else can understand what has already been done and pick up from there.

Anticipating what a user might do and providing for all logical contingencies is the job of the software designer. If an input of zero could result in a divide by zero somewhere, this eventually should be checked for and trapped by the program which would then issue an appropriate message. Nothing is more frustrating to a user unfamiliar with the details of programming than to enter a program and get back as the only response either a blank screen or some system message gibberish which might as well be in Sanskrit.

6.4.5 Language Suitability for Simulation

Whether the software produced has the desired characteristics described above or not is mainly dependent on the competence of the modeler and programmer, but is also somewhat dependent on the programming language used. To produce good simulation software, the language itself should have the following language characteristics:

Desirable for developer	Desirable for user
D1. Perform needed operations conveniently	U1. Good input/output including graphics
D2. Allow modularity	
D3. Self documenting	U3. Fast
D4. Transportable	
D5. Easily maintained and updated	
D6. Character manipulation	
D7. Versatile input/output	

Based on the desirable characteristics of a language given above, a subjective comparison of the suitability of various languages for simulation can be prepared. One such is presented in Table 6.2.

A short discussion will amplify some of the advantages and disadvantages of various languages.

APL

APL has the advantages of being both powerful and interactive. However, its terse, dense language consisting of Greek letters, mathematical symbols, and some symbols not normally used by the general technical community makes it what some refer to as a "write only" language. As a potential language for writing simulation software it has two disadvantages: (1) it is an interpretive language, which means it will compute slower than a compiled or assembled language; and (2), by far the more serious drawback, it is difficult to maintain significant programs with potentially thousands of lines of code. The original programmer will have difficulty understanding APL statements he wrote himself after a few weeks or months, and these same statements will be virtually impossible for other programmers and analysts to decipher. The language is at once powerful, elegant, concise, but too obscure to recommend it for all but the simplest simulations.

C

The language C is a powerful one developed at Bell Laboratories in conjunction with an operating system called Unix. It is something like an advanced assembly language but much easier to learn. It too has the

Table 6.2 Suitability of Languages for Simulation[a]

Language	Characteristic									
	D1	D2	D3	D4	D5	D6	D7	U1	U2	U3
APL	F	G	P	F	P	G	F	G	F	F
BASIC	F	P	F	G	G	G	F	G	F	P
CSMP	Dynamics	P	F	F	F	N	F	N	F	G
GPSS	Stochastic	P	P	N	F	N	F	N	P	P
SIMULA	F	G	F	F	F	P	P	N	F	G
FORTRAN	F	G	F	G	G	P	F	N	F	G
PL1	F	G	F	P	F	F	F	N	F	F
ASSEMBLY	G	G	F	N	P	G	G	G	G	G
PASCAL	F	G	G	F	G	G	G	G	G	G

[a]G = good; F = fair; P = poor; N = none.

drawback of readability. While it enjoys popularity, some might say fanatical support, from a group of users primarily involved in developing operating systems, it will probably never be a popular language in which to develop simulations.

PL1

The PL1 language has most of the features desirable for developing simulation software, except for being interactive. In the past, it had an enormous amount of overhead associated with its compile and link steps, was implemented fully only on IBM computers, and was implemented rather halfheartedly on non-IBM mainframes. In addition, documentation was hard to read and difficult to find. It is now available on personal computers and, except for its interactive limitations and lack of inherent graphics capabilities, will undoubtedly gain in popularity.

Pascal

This theoretically conceived and designed language lends itself to logical thinking and straightforward structures in software. Its input/output handling is somewhat primitive, especially as implemented on personal computers, but for small-scale simulations, it has good potential.

Pascal is the precursor to another more powerful language, also developed by Niklaus Wirth, in which most of Pascals deficiencies have been corrected. This new language is called Modula 2. It is not yet widely available nor is its documentation. But when it becomes better distributed and known it will provide a very good vehicle for developing simulations. As it increases in popularity it will ultimately overshadow and swallow up its little brother, Pascal.

ADA

The language, developed to be the programming language for the Department of Defense, is too complex to be transportable. The complexity, in terms of many bells and whistles, also precludes it being implemented on minicomputers and personal computers. Subsets of ADA, Augusta and Janus, are currently too limited in their functions to be of general use and are primarily of academic and special-use interest.

6.5 DOCUMENTATION

Not enough positive attention has been given to software documentation. Even IBM, the giant of the computer industry, has produced and continues to produce disorganized, poorly written, incompletely indexed, and uninteresting documentation for its software. Originally the problem lay with the programmers who were interested only in creating successful software. But now the burden of guilt rests upon the managers of software development. They at least should know better.

Table 6.3 presents a list of 14 characteristics for good software documentation; they are discussed below. The first eight of these are necessary both for the user and for programmer reference. The remaining six complete the minimum requirements for programmer documentation.

1. Narrative description tells a prospective user enough for him to decide if the software attacks the problem he wants to solve. The narrative should be on two levels of detail: an abstract and a detailed description.

2. Input and output are the actual interfaces between the user and the computer. If input requirements are difficult, too voluminous, or inconvenient to use (such as mixed English and metric units), potential users will be put off. Similarly, output must be reasonable in format and volume. Textual material that is all uppercase, for instance, is difficult to read. With today's technology, there is no excuse for such output.

Table 6.3 Minimum Characteristics for Good Software Documentation

	User	Programmer	Documentation
1.	x	x	Narrative description of what the program does, methods
2.	x	x	Sample I/O[a]
3.	x	x	I/O description and units
4.	x	x	Input data error trapping and messages
5.	x	x	Data file organization and layout
6.	x	x	References
7.	x	x	Mathematical model that program is based upon
8.	x	x	Record of program developmental/revisions
9.		x	Names of all subroutines involved
10.		x	Program listing
11.		x	Glossary of variables
12.		x	Flow charts
13.		x	Correspondence and written comments about software
14.	x	x	Test case with complete I/O

[a]I/O = Input/output.

3. The input data requirements must be completely described. Frequently, different cases require different amounts of information organized in different ways.

4. If there are limits on the sizes of various parameters or specific regions which cause problems for the program, these should be clearly stated. Optional units for both input and output and how these options are invoked are required information.

5. For applications involving large collections of data, it is necessary to describe not only what data are in the data base, but how it is organized. Some applications might be precluded by, for instance, a hierarchical structure.

6. Sometimes, a useful algorithm is programmed and used for several years before it is superceded by further developments. Without pertinent references it is frequently very difficult or impossible to determine the origin of an algorithm just from the program coding.

7. Many different approaches and mathematical models are possible for any given system. The exact mathematical model the program is based upon must be given. Without such a description, it is not possible to verify that the program does in fact faithfully represent the model it is supposed to.

8. A useful program can and does "live" over a period of years. Each modification to a program must be faithfully noted so that efforts to rerun bench marks or test cases can be duplicated, or any differences between current results and earlier runs be explained.

9. A list of the names of all subprograms is required in order to assure proper maintenance. If a subroutine used by several programs resides in a central file, changes transparent to one user might adversely affect another. In addition to knowing what subroutines are called by a given main program, it is sometimes necessary to know what main programs call a given subroutine.

10. An up-to-date listing is always required before any work can be done on a program. Much time has been wasted chasing bugs with listings full of red revision marks, not all of them up to date.

11. Glossaries provide a quick reference to those not familiar with a given problem area. They also state explicit definitions where conflicting or nebulous meanings are possible.

12. Flow charts are indispensable. Even the simplest logic requires a diagram. When the logic is presented graphically, as in a flow diagram, it is relatively easy to understand how an algorithm works. Having a logically consistent and complete algorithm is an absolute necessity before programming begins and indispensable for later maintenance and update. As mentioned briefly earlier, the level of detail of a flow chart should be enough to show the logic or order of processing but not so detailed that the forest cannot be discerned because of the trees. For particularly complex parts of the algorithm, there can and should be two levels of detail: one general and one detailed.

13. A chronicle of correspondence concerning the software will help retain the reasons for its development, any problems and their solutions, and any unusual uses of the program. Such documentation will aid in updating and enhancing the software package and provide a written rationale for its current status.

14. Test cases which exercise all of the options in a program and for which correct answers are known are very useful and valuable. They provide a means to validate the software, to compare the results from using different methods, and to compare execution times.

As a final note on documentation, it is worth reiterating the point that the finest program in the world is practically useless to all but its author if it is not documented properly.

6.6 SOFTWARE DEVELOPMENT

Existing software packages should be used when they are available and applicable. However, it often happens that a simulation package does not exist for the application under study. To perform the simulation under these circumstances some software will have to be developed.

Software development is a significant task requiring long-term commitments and with long-term repercussions. It is not to be undertaken lightly. Criteria for determining the mode of software procurement should be established to help choose between: buying off the shelf, buying off the shelf and modifying in-house, having a software house develop, and developing in-house.

If any in-house effort is involved, the following section on managing software development should prove useful. Regardless of the source of the software, it will have to be tested as discussed in Section 6.7.

6.6.1 Managing Software Development

The management functions of organizing, planning, motivating, and controlling can be put to good use in the area of software development.

One effective organization is to assign chief programmers to specific functions and have them choose a programming team to meet the specified needs. Each team works on a segment of the software and uses standardized nomenclature and structures to ease the burden of interfacing the various independently written segments into a cohesive operating package.

This approach requires careful planning to (1) develop the overall structure, (2) to divide the responsibilities between the programming teams, and (3) to interface and test the final product.

Development is always an iterative process. Structured walk throughs can be presented periodically so that the potential users can see what developments are complete at a certain time and to help refine the ongoing effort. In addition, the contact between user and software developer will help motivate members of the programming team.

The programming teams should be given a set of standardized coding conventions, all should use structured programming [1], of which top-down programming is one example, and should adhere to a uniform software development system [2].

Documents #1—#10 mentioned below provide the specifications to use in performing the control function. Adherence to answering the questions posed in the project definition phase will assure a successful project.

Definition Phase

Most projects begin as the response to a stated need or as a solution to a stated problem. Invariably, the initial statement of the problem is in a primitive form such as "A fire hydrant will have to be installed to handle the possibility of fires in the new section of the plant." The response to this primitive problem statement can take the form of possible alternates, i.e., more specific problems.

> *Alt. 1* Extend the nearest existing service water line and ter-minate it at the edge of the new section of the plant for fire-fighting.

> *Alt. 2* Determine the height of the tallest structure in the new section and determine how much pressure would be required to reach the top of it and the volume of water most likely required to put out a fire there.

> *Alt. 3* Design the pipes and pumps required to deliver 1000 gal-lons per minute of water to any section of the new plant.

The solutions to these and many more specific problems might satisfy the actual need implied by the original primitive problem. The engineer must determine which specific problem, when solved, will best meet the needs of the primitive problem.

This synthesis of plausible alternative problems is the first and most critical task the engineer must do to solve the original problem. Which questions really need to be answered?

Model feasibility study—Document #1 The document in the defini-tion phase must answer the questions about whether a computer model can be produced which will answer the questions settled on, at a cost-effective price. The feasibility study should clearly define the system to be modified and explicitly state the questions to be answered. In addition, it should clearly state what the criteria for a successful project will be. It should describe what resources will be necessary to produce the second document, the system model, and indicate how long it will take to produce. This includes data gathering and analysis.

The chronology of producing the system model will be useful in preparing the resource plan.

System model—Document #2 The system model is the fundamental working document for the entire project. All other work relates to it in some way. It must include all explicit assumptions and all mathematical and logical relationships, and be complete enough so that, given time, a person could arrive at the answer to all of the questions raised in the feasibility study by solving the equations and logical relationships.

Project proposal—Document #3 Once the adequacy of the system has been agreed to, the form the computer model is to take can be developed and planned. A general outline of the computer model design must be prepared. The project proposal then addresses the questions:

1. What can be accomplished with the computer model?

2. What is the value of what it will do?

3. How much will it cost to produce, in time, money, and manpower?

Design Phase

Having completed the system model during the definition phase, the computer model can now be designed (this assumes that an acceptable project proposal, document #3, has been approved by management).

Computer model design specifications—Document #4 Working from the system model and the project proposal (Documents #2 and #3), qualified members of the team should specify exactly how the computer program will be structured. If this document were given to a programmer, it should be reasonable to expect him to produce one module of the overall system and have it mesh with others. The general architecture developed in the project proposal is to be fleshed out to include a detailed description of:

1. What type input is to be accommodated. This might include one or more of the following: cards, keyboard, tape, disk, fixed field, free form, oral, interactive, CRT, or light pen.

2. What type output is desired. This might consist of any or all of the following: cards, tape, disk, CRT, tables, graphs, plots, text, oral, or specific report formats.

3. Which parts of the system model will be handled by which computer software module. Associated with each software module will be a description of the verification tests which must run in order to demonstrate the module performs its required function.

Programmer's handbook—Document #5 This describes any conditions to which everyone involved in programming must adhere. This should include:

1. All naming conventions for variables, COMMONs, subroutines

2. Coding conventions such as when FUNCTION subroutines are allowable, whether to use FORTRAN, Assembler language, Algol, etc.

3. Internal units for variables, such as, in the English system, lengths in feet, time in hours, mass in pounds, etc.

4. Documentation requirements, i.e., exactly how much and what documentation is required for each module

5. Change procedure:
   a. Under what conditions a programmer can initiate a change in the computer model design specifications
   b. Who should receive notification of the changes
   c. How the changes will be identified, cataloged, and kept track of (formalized, dated, and numbered change memos, are a good example)
   d. Who is to review and approve any proposed changes

Programming, Verification, and Validation Phase

Using all of the information from Documents #1–#5, the main document is produced in this phase: the computer model. However, in going from the design specifications to an implemented model, if any changes in specifications are necessary or desirable, these changes can be achieved through change memos.

Change memos—Document #6 As mentioned above, hindsight is better than foresight. During the implementation of the computer model it will become obvious that some previously specified items: (1) must be changed, or (2) would be highly desireable to change.

When such changes are formally agreed upon, Change Memos are issued to all concerned giving:

1. The reasons for the change

2. The date of the changes

3. The changes to be made

4. How the changes might impact future activities in the project

There might be more than one change memo; there might be none. These memos will be issued at unspecified times and will be collected right up until the project is completed. The collected change memos will constitute document #6.

Computer model—Document #7 The computer listing of the completed and debugged computer model is only part of Docuement #7.
The computer model should be developed in a modular fashion. As
each module is verified, it should be documented. Finally, when the
individual modules are integrated into a complete system, verification
runs should show this too.

Validation tests belong here as well, showing what the real system data are and how the model results compare. Any bench mark
simulations used to verify or validate should be included.

User's handbook—Document #8 The program developer might not
always be the person who will want to use it. Consequently, the
user's handbook should be prepared so that someone relatively familiar
with the problem area but totally unfamiliar with the computer model
can sit down with the handbook and fire up the system to simulate a
desired case or cases.

As a bare minimum the handbook should include:

1. Brief statement of what the program does

2. Method of solution

3. Expected results

4. Computer to run on and language used

5. Input data required

6. Error messages

7. Unusual quirks of the system

8. Constraints

9. Output formats

10. Options and how to invoke them

11. Expected execution time or method to estimate it

More details on user documentation are given in Section 5.4.

Operational Phase

Before this phase is implemented, the program will have been validated
and verified per Section 6.7. Plans for performing the simulation runs
should be laid out in advance so that all of the original questions mentioned in the project proposal can be answered. Frequently, other
questions will arise as the simulation proceeds and runs will be added
to help answer these newly raised questions.

By now, the project has been carried on for several weeks or
months. Information summarizing the progress and status of the
project should be gathered and organized.

Simulation results—Document #9 This report will include the plan for the simulation runs, the results of each individual run, any conclusions from an analysis of the results, and recommendations concerning further runs.

Wrapup Phase

A summary report of the entire project will be prepared during this phase.

Project summary report—Document #10 This report will summarize the rationale, progress, results, conclusions, costs, and benefits of the project, and evaluate it against the criteria for success established during the design phase. Recommendations for further work will also be included here.

There is a deliberate emphasis on documentation in this section, to reinforce the material in Section 6.5. Many organizations have ignored or delayed the proper documentation of software until driven to the wall by necessity. By then, the original authors of the programs are gone or otherwise unavailable and many facets of the software remain undocumented and perhaps unused. Giving documentation short shrift is a sure path to rapid software obsolescence.

6.7 SOFTWARE TESTING

The main objectives of testing are: (1) to verify that the computer program truly reflects the mathematical model, (2) to validate the computer results against the real system it is supposed to represent, and (3) to determine if there is conformity between the program and the published documentation, especially the user's manual and the programmer's manual.

A complete Basic language listing of the modified Hardy Cross procedure for an Apple II+ computer is given in Appendix A. This program was used to run data corresponding to network #2 described in Ingels and Powers [4]. The results of the validation run are summarized in Table 6.4.

The maximum difference is 0.24% in pipe #1. This is insignificant and could be accounted for by differences in the number of bits used to represent numbers and perform floating-point arithmetic.

The conclusion is thus reached that the program adequately represents the equations and the equations reproduce previously published results. There is no actual performance data to check against for our hypothetical plant, but, from the check above, we expect the program to provide a reasonable representation of the real world.

Table 6.4 Validation of Modified Hardy Cross

Pipe flow		Flow program	Difference	Percent difference
No.	Ref. 4			
1	435.85	436.90	1.05	0.24
2	227.60	227.65	0.05	0.02
3	258.32	258.26	0.06	0.02
4	123.40	123.47	0.07	0.06
5	142.75	142.88	0.13	0.09
6	134.92	134.79	0.13	0.10
7	65.50	65.37	0.13	0.20

Verification of the program vis á vis the mathematical model is best carried out by testing each module individually. Any equations, constraints, or logic can be tested using temporary drivers for specific modules.

Debugging aids are widely available for most operating systems now and can be used effectively during the verification phase. The top-down approach will assure that as individual modules are cleaned up, they will fit into the overall scheme.

It is also during this testing phase that error trapping for bad data is implemented and checked. There should be a standard procedure initiated when any error in data is discovered by the program. This is often accomplished by assigning an error number and calling a central error-handling routine which issues messages, determines if the error is fatal, and whether the data screening can profitably be continued.

Validating the program against the real world system requires data from the actual system. It is not uncommon for the data to be difficult or expensive to obtain and, once obtained, to have so much "scatter" in them that it is not obvious whether unconformities lie in the scatter or in the models inadequacies. Such real phenomena require an organized, statistically sound data collection procedure, usually based upon design of experiments methodology.

If serious discrepencies occur between the computer results and the real system data that cannot be accounted for because of scatter, the model is implicated and another iteration of improvement starting all the way back with model development will have to be initiated.

During validation testing, bench-mark cases are very helpful. Such cases can provide optional data for both interpolation between known data points and extrapolation into regions of interest. Cases with limiting values for parameters can be used in validating, too,

especially if the real system is known to approach some value
asymptotically.

REFERENCES

1. Jensen, R. W., *I.E.E.E. Computers*, *14*(3):31—50 (1981).
2. Bergeland, C. D., "A Guided Tour of Program Design Method-
   ologies", *I.E.E.E. Computers*, *14*(10):13—37 (1981).
3. Hadley, G., *Linear Programming*, Addison-Wesley, 1972.
4. Ingels, D. M., and J. E. Powers, "Analysis of Pipeline Networks", *C.E.P.*, Feb. 1964, pp. 65—70.
5. Bennett, W. S. and C. F. Everet, Jr., *What Every Engineer
   Should Know About Microcomputers: Hardware/Software Design: A Step-by-Step Example*, Marcel Dekker, Inc., N.Y.,
   1980.
6. Olujic, Z., "Computer Friction Factors Fast for Flow in Pipes,"
   Chem. Eng., Dec. 14, 1981, pp. 91—93.

7

SIMULATION

*Give to any hypothesis which is worth your while to consider
just that degree of credence which the evidence warrants.*

[Bertrand Russell]

7.1 INTRODUCTION

The following provide motivation for performing simulation studies:
(1) safety, (2) cost, (3) extrapolation, (4) ease of modification,
(5) sensitivity studies, (6) optimization/ameliorization, (7) lack of
alternatives, (8) increased knowledge of system, and (9) the solving
of classes of problems.

Safety is of paramount importance under circumstances in which
the lives or health of people might be in jeopardy or expensive equipment might be in danger. The manned space program provides an
example of both. Not only are the astronauts' welfare on the line
every time a mission is attempted, but so are millions of dollars worth
of equipment. Many aspects of this effort are simulated over and over
assuming different conditions, malfunctions, etc., so that contingency
planning to protect the men and equipment can be effective. With the
exception of the fire which cost the lives of one crew, the approach
has been highly successful.

Even if equipment is not damaged during an event, it might be
very expensive to conduct. The cost of a large-scale military operation,

for example, is enormous. As a result, the senior officers spend a lot of time performing war games, i.e., simulations of large-scale military maneuvers, so that they can be exposed to many possible situations without spending all of the money necessary to have a live operation. Similar circumstances pertain to industrial operations where much sharper eyes are kept on cost than the military traditionally does.

Operating data provide base case and bench mark information for adjusting parameters in the simulation model. Once these tuning parameters are set to fit existing data, the model can be used to explore operating conditions which have not yet been encountered by the actual system. The excursions away from collected data can be either interpolative moves or exorapolations.

Interpolative moves by a model will usually fairly represent the actual system if the parameter tuning was successful. However, depending upon the nature of the model, extrapolation can produce results that are anything from highly accurate to totally unreliable. In particular, if the model uses statistical curve fitting, especially polynomials, to represent the fundamental relationships between variables, extrapolation is not to be relied upon. If, on the other hand, the model is a set of fundamental relationships based upon known physical laws, such as the mass, energy, and momentum balances, there is some hope that extrapolation will at least produce a result that has the right general trend. This exemplifies the principle that it behooves the engineer to be familiar with the fundamentals of the simulation model so that he can use it effectively.

Models, and computer models especially, have the happy property that they can be readily modified. This provides opportunities to compare alternate theories about the underlying relationships. Equations of state provide a good example of a set of competing relationship which might be evaluated for use in a study. Some equations of state are best used only for gases at relatively high temperatures. Some equations of state are known to be poor in the region of the critical point of a material. No equation of state is best under all conditions or all materials. The result is that several might be tried out before a selection is made. Such modifications are easily done with simulation models. Frequently, such options are built into the simulation program.

Sensitivity studies indicate the rate at which one variable changes with the changes in a second variable. It is quite useful to know that the value of a certain variable can be changed, say 20%, before it appreciably affects another one. Or, if it is discovered that some variables are completely insensitive to changes in the major variables, perhaps the model can be simplified by omitting references to the insensitive variables. Such studies can also be used to check out the model. If it is known that variable A affects variable B but the simulation runs do not reflect such an effect, then the model must be modified or its validity reevaluated.

One of the major aims of any engineering study should be to determine how best to accomplish a given task. This implies some form of optimization. A simulation model, no matter how large and complex, can be treated as a black box system which is supplied inputs for certain variables and which, from these, generates output variables. Any such black box system can be attacked using a wide range of optimization techniques that can operate with only input—output values.

However, some simulations take so much computer time for each run—such as a compositional, three-dimensional, multiformation reservoir steam flood—that it is too expensive to run an optimization study to completion. Under such circumstances, the guiding principle is amelioration. If the best answer can't be found, at least find one better than the current one. This emphasizes the need for simulation software to have restart-continuation capability so that such studies can carry on from where they left off.

Several factors, including the cost of real system modification, safety, and current knowledge of the system, might leave no alternate way to forecast the effects of changes in a system other than through simulation. Forecasting the effects of astronomical events, such as the passing of a Halley's comet, is an example of such a situation.

If the simulation study is properly conducted, with good planning and by posing meaningful questions to be answered, etc., it will lead to increased knowledge of the system. The sensitivity studies might indicate rules of thumb that were not obvious or they might indicate that the model hypothesized is inadequate. In either case, useful information will have been obtained. By its very nature, developing a computer model requires gaining insight into the phenomena under study.

Another highly beneficial facet of simulation software is that, if the modeling equations can be cast in terms of basic physical principles, then the program will simulate an entire class of systems. For example, the program to simulate a distillation tower can be written so that by inputing values for the composition of the feed, the operating pressure and temperature, and the physical parameters (such as number of trays and their spacing), not just one tower can be simulated, but a whole class of towers. The additional work to make the software cover a certain class of problems is small relative to the benefits gained, but this approach must be anticipated and planned for during model development. There are now many software packages which can simulate the steady-state operation of entire petrochemical plants. These packages have solved the class of problems which might be described as the steady-state operation of any configuration of interconnected unit operations of the given types for the given list of materials. The list of unit operations and materials would then be given along with some maximum number of units that the program could handle in one plant.

It is this generality, or ability to simulate an entire class of systems, which indicates the power for the computer modeling and simulation approach. No other method has the versatility, cost advantage, and ease of updating represented by this approach.

For irreversible, time-dependent systems such as petroleum reservoirs, the real system can and will have only one actual performance. It is not repeatable or reversible. It can only be produced one time. Experimentation with such systems can be prohibitive in both time and expense. For such systems, simulation runs are relatively inexpensive and can produce results quickly. They can be run over and over switching various operating regimes to determine how best to operate the real reservoir or field. The timing of crucial operations, such as when to initiate water flooding, how often to perform huff and puff thermal injection, and what well pattern and spacing to use, can be determined.

The tools of simulation range from the mental model or judgement of individual engineers to the complex mathematical models programmed for computers. The question for complex systems such as petroleum reservoirs is not whether to use simulation but what kind of simulation to use.

Assuming that the modeling work has been done and the computer program has been verified against the model and validated with some real data, simulation consists of five phases: (1) developing a well-defined statement of objectives including a list of what questions are to be answered, (2) collecting pertinent input data and evaluating it, (3) exercising the program to produce results which will help attain the objectives set in phase 1, (4) analyzing the results obtained, and (5) producing a report of the simulation study, its results, conclusions and recommendations. As with the modeling effort, simulation is frequently iterative in nature. Upon exercising the program it is often discovered that either the list of questions was wrong or incomplete. Not infrequently, after one complete pass through phases 1 to 4, it is determined that the problem definition and objectives were insufficient or inappropriate; the wrong system was studied. When such a situation obtains, another complete iteration is called for.

As an example of solving the wrong problem, Albert Bressand [1] recently wrote: "Thus we are straining to overcome an international economic crisis through national economic policies. Models of closed national economies still govern much of our thinking, and we wonder with incredulity at their failure—be it Keynesian or on the monetary side." In other words, the problems of an economy that is structurally part of the international economic system can't be solved by simulating only a national economy.

7.2 PROBLEM DEFINITION PHASE

The problem to be studied should be delineated clearly by a written statement of objectives and a corresponding list of questions for which answers are sought. A great deal of wasted time is spent generating simulation results which don't help answer the questions that need to be answered, usually because they haven't been asked. It's not uncommon to take as the initial statement of a problem some nebulous directive such as: "Simulate the landing of the craft from the lunar orbiter on the moon." Specifically, what does that mean? Is fuel consumption of concern, or craft orientation, landing velocity, control mechanism behavior, interior temperature, trajectory, a pilot's field of vision? These primitive problem statements must be restated as specifically as possible.

A good set of user documentation will indicate the limits of applicability for the variables and the methods used in the model, so that a determination can be made before the simulation is commenced of whether the program is suitable for meeting the objectives of the study. The more specific the objectives are, the more likely that they can be met.

To properly conduct the simulation, the engineer must have some knowledge of how the model is formulated and use his judgement while setting up the runs. The formulation of the model will affect three important characteristics of the simulation which will be of great interest to the engineer: (1) stability, (2) accuracy, and (3) cost.

Stability is affected by several things, but an overriding one is the mode of representation of any differential equations. Numerical representation of differential equations can be explicit, implicit, or some mixture as mentioned in Chapter 4. The more implicit the solution procedure, the more stable it is. This stability is usually paid for with some increase in computation time. If a simulation package has stability problems and it is formulated in the explicit mode, consideration should be given to finding or developing an implicit procedure.

Accuracy is affected by truncation error, time step size, and grid spacing. Unless a new formulation is under consideration, the user does not have much control over truncation error other than through normalizing variables so they are all of the same order of magnitude. However, the time step size and grid spacing can be manipulated to balance off accuracy versus computation time. A good test case or bench mark problem similar to the problem at hand is useful in finding a reasonable time step size and grid spacing. Of course, many software packages can automatically adjust the spacing as computation progresses and do not require such intervention on the part of the user.

The cost of the simulation depends on all of the factors mentioned above: stability, time step size, grid spacing, and problem formulation.

Decreases in step size or grid spacing usually increase the accuracy, but, at the same time, increase the cost due to additional storage requirements and longer computation times. This conflict between increased accuracy and higher costs must be dealt with by the engineer through problem definition and by balancing out requirements for accuracy and stability.

While defining the problem to answer the basic questions posed, consideration should be given to planning the simulation runs using statistical techniques from the design of experiments area. A well-planned set of runs will maximize the useful information obtained in a small number of runs and add to the confidence in the validity of the conclusions drawn. It will also frequently save both time and money and lead to keener insights into the system being simulated.

7.3 DATA INPUT PHASE

In addition to gathering data for the parameters required by the program, data must be gathered about the performance of the real system. Many simulation programs require not only a set of input data for the conditions under study, but a set of response data from which adjustable parameter values are determined. Such a base case simulation provides no new information for the user. It is necessary so that model parameters can be tuned to the specific system being simulated, and is commonly referred to as "performance matching" or "history matching."

For cases in which a general algorithm has been developed with adjustable parameters, a wide variety or a complete class of systems can be attacked with the same software.

When the input data requirements are heavy, such as for petroleum reservoir simulations, collecting the data, verifying their correctness and consistency, and entering the data into the computer represent significant manpower demands. Such large-scale simulations tend to provide for automatically saving the input so that future runs will require only modifying those data that have changed from a previous case.

The basic data for simulation tend to fall into several categories: problem topology, process parameters and operating conditions, numerical procedures data, calculation order, data limits, data storage information, and unit conversions. Each of these will be discussed below.

The problem topology data describe how various subsystems are related to each other. For electric circuits they would describe which elements were in loops together and which loops were connected. For chemical plants or refineries it would indicate such things as the order of processing units. The incidence matrix and other graph theory

techniques discussed in Chapter 4 are some of the tools used to describe and analyze topology.

Process parameters and operating conditions specify sizes, capa-
cities, orientations, properties, and, if pertinent, conditions such as
pressure, temperature, and humidity. Simulations involving a large
number of material components, such as for petroleum reservoirs, often
require laboratory data to specify general properties (like specific
gravity, viscosity, and refractive index) about the material, the actual
composition being unknown, from which other properties are inferred
or estimated.

In addition to time step size and grid spacing, other numerical
procedure data might be required such as convergence tolerence,
maximum iterations allowed, specification of which option to use for
a numerical technique, and rejection limits for history matching. These
parameters have a material effect on accuracy and computation time.
They should be varied early in the simulation runs to determine suitable values for the bulk of the computation which will ensue.

Many systems are composed of interconnected subsystems com-
prising some type of network. Convergence of networks entails what
can be referred to as "recycle" computations. The rate at which convergence is attained for a network is affected by the order of computation for the subsystems. Most sophisticated simulation packages contain algorithms for automatically handling the problem, but these general methods are not always the most efficient. Any special knowledge
the engineer has about the order of computation which will be most
effective should be transmitted to the simulation package if possible.
This usually takes the form of a preferred order of calculation for the
subsystems.

Data limits can frequently be provided by the user. These are
minima and maxima beyond which certain parameters don't make sense
for the current simulation. Such limits can be fruitfully used not only
at data input time, but during the calculation phase as well. For simulations in which each run can take a significant amount of computer
time, it is worthwhile to abort runs that have obviously gone awry and
from which the only indication is that the results have exceeded the
reasonable limits set by the user.

Simulations which handle large amounts of data sometimes provide
options for both where input data are to be obtained and which files
are to be allocated for output. Data management flexibility can be
useful for handling temporary output and intermediate results, for
running continuations and ad hoc simulations, etc. It is achieved at
the cost of additional knowledge requirements on the part of the user.

With the interwoven world economy of today, it is highly desirable
to have the computer software handle unit conversions between various
systems. In the United States it is common to have English engineering
units and some form of metric units. With just these two systems, the

Software must handle four possibilities: English in with either English or metric out, and metric in with either metric or English out. Good engineering design practice precludes having mixed English and metric input or output.

7.4 PREPROCESSING PHASE

Much of the preprocessing activity is transparent to the user, but it behooves him to be aware of what is going on. For some simulators this activity is limited to data checking. For others, it can involve compiling, link-editing, data fitting, switch setting, and data retrieval from archives, in addition to data checking.

Simulators which solve a class of problems may have what amounts to a library of computer routines, each routine representing a particular unit in the system to be simulated. Because the total number of such routines can be quite large, it is convenient to link together only those that are needed for a particular simulation run. This is accomplished by reading in topology data and generating a program which only calls the pertinent routines. Since a program is generated, it must be compiled and link-edited with the pertinent routines. ASPEN [2] and PRODYC [3] are examples of simulation packages which operate in this fashion.

Obtaining the physical and thermodynamic properties of various materials which might be in a simulation run at each different condition can consume large amounts of computer time. It is possible and it has occurred that general materials property packages have been implemented and used by simulators. For a large fraction of applications, the amount of computer time spent calculating material properties can exceed the time spent computing everything else. This is a consequence of using a general properties routine for every computation. As an alternative, it is possible, and some simulators have the capability, to determine during the preprocessor phase the materials involved and the range of conditions they will be subjected to, and from the general properties package generate a set of property points spanning the range of interest. These points are then used to prepare simple property curves through data fitting, resulting in efficient computational expressions.

Another form of data fitting is also performed by some simulation packages. Raw data from the real system can be supplied for part of the performance-matching activity. Specific forms of equations are used with statistical curve-fitting procedures to prepare maximum likelihood parameters to represent the real data. The forms of the equations used for curve fitting are the same forms used by the simulation program. For example, there are several equations for representing viscosity, but if raw data were supplied, the simulation package would

calculate parameters to fit the form of the viscosity equations which
the simulator normally uses. This frees the engineer from finding a
reasonable equational form for viscosity and knowing how to perform
the statistical curve fitting.

For large simulators which have several possible computational
paths, such as those for petroleum reservoirs, the computational sequence of portions of the simulation can be selected by the user. This
is done by the engineer by indicating options through the input data.
These options are then used to set software switches which control
the path of the computational sequence.

Data is a corporate resource. During the design of a plant or
facility an enormous amount of information is generated. If it is properly identified, indexed, and stored, it can provide a wealth of pertinent
data not only during the phase of the project during which it was generated, but for future operations and subsequent facilities. Computer-
aided design through the use of models and simulations can also generate voluminous results. Such data should be stored on some secondary media, such as magnetic tape, after its active project has been completed, so that it can be retrieved for future reference. Long-term
trends and historically significant shifts can sometimes be discerned
by reviewing archived data of this type.

Simulation runs that are continuations of previous runs or which
are compilations of several previous runs can draw the data from the
archives and prepare it for further use during the preprocessor phase.

7.5 CALCULATION PHASE

Performance matching can relate to both steady-state and time-varying
parameter adjustment. History matching consists of adjusting the parameters until simulated performance trends match observed trends the
ultimate aim being to forecast future performance. Such history matching is usually most effective for deterministic systems. However, some
stochastic processes, such as presidential elections, have been history
matched and with a small amount of current data have enjoyed success
in predicting the outcome of what is essentially a nondeterministic
process. Such parameter adjustment takes place early in a simulation
study, frequently in the preprocessor phase (if one exists).

Some properties are known with a greater degree of accuracy than
others. In reservoir simulation, for example, for a given composition,
the properties of the fluids involved are known relatively better than
the reservoir formation properties such as permeability, porosity, and
capillary pressure. It is important to know the relative accuracy of
the variables affecting the simulation so that results can be properly
evaluated and so that proper decisions can be made regarding where
to put additional effort to significantly improve the quality of the

results. If fluid properties are known to be within plus or minus 5% of their true values and permeability to be only within plus or minus 25%, it would not make sense to spend any additional effort on getting better results for fluid properties.

The desirable attributes a simulation program should have to make it most useful during the calculation phase are:

Validity

Ease of use

Versatility

Efficient computation

Generality

If software is to be acquired or developed, these should be kept in mind.

Validity has been stressed several times before. One of the oldest sayings in computer lore comes to mind: "garbage in—garbage out." If the model or the data have not been validated the results probably won't be worth much.

User friendliness has been mentioned before too. When a significant study is to be undertaken, the easier the simulator is to use, the more likely the outcome will be as desired. Hair shirts, with the hairy side in, went out of style with the medieval monastaries that spawned them. Good simulation software provides an interface that allows a person who is not a computer specialist to make significant use of it without undue suffering.

Programs which solve a class of problems or simulate an entire class of systems tend to be versatile. Not only can complete systems be studied, but subunits can be studied as well. Sometimes the materials properties part of the software is available without requiring any simulation. Making the various components of a simulation package available requires considerable forethought. If such versatility exists, it is a sign of well-planned software. Providing calculating versatility makes the job of the user that much simpler. Instead of needing to know how to interface with one package for thermodynamic properties, another package for curve fitting, and still another for networking processes, he can learn one versatile system and more effectively do his job.

Computational efficiency is the second most important attribute, after validity. It is the user's responsibility to investigate the numerical methods parameters and alternative calculational sequences to establish an efficient simulation. This assumes that the software developer has done his job properly by generating effective code.

There will be some trade-off between generality and efficiency. The more general a software package, the more nonproductive overhead it must have in it. The general operating system, OS360 (for the IBM 360 computer) provides a case in point. It was conceived of and implemented as an operating system which would be general enough to handle the full spectrum of activities for the computer. It did indeed function as intended. The problem with it was that it was cumbersome. A simple job which might require only one-tenth of a second to execute, required two seconds to be set up by the operating system. The overhead was more than an order of magnitude larger than the productive computation time. Nevertheless, it provided a single interface which, if mastered, eliminated most of the confusion of how to get the computer system to respond in a desired manner.

A simulation system doesn't exist which is general enough to simulate everything. What do exist are programs which simulate a class of systems, as mentioned earlier, and general simulation languages which ease the burden of translating models into computer programs. If a series of simulations are planned, the preferred approach would be to find a simulation package which handled the particular class of systems under study.

One of the aims of engineers is to find better ways of doing things and, if economical and feasible, to find the best way of doing a specific task. Optimization studies can be readily conducted using simulation techniques. It is usually possible to embed a simulation package within the optimization process. The optimization software will then generate the values of the input variables, and pass these to the simulation package which will generate the values for the output variables. The optimization package will then take the inputs and their corresponding output and generate a new set of inputs to pass to the simulator. The simulation software is thus nothing more than a black box as far as the optimization program is concerned. Inputs are fed to the black box which then provides the outputs corresponding to these inputs. The process is continued until an optimum has been attained or some limiting resource such as time, money, or manpower has been consumed.

Two points about optimization must be emphasized. First, for multivariable problems optimization methods only seek a local optimum. A series of starting points might thus have to be used to explore the possibility of the existence of more than one local optimum, only one of which will be the global optimum. Second, if there are a large number of variables involved (10 is plenty large) and the problem cannot be treated via linear programming, the computation time for each simulation run might be so long that even a local optimum is not reached because of the exhaustion of a resource such as available time. The optimization process is thus not completed and the engineer will have to settle for amelioration, i.e., making the situation better (since best has not yet been attained).

Special care must always be taken in defining the objective function and constraints for an optimization problem. Frequently, in those
situations which are most interesting, there are competing effects that
are sought, such as maximizing profit while at the same time minimizing
the expenditure of certain resources.

7.6 OUTPUT PHASE

Good simulators provide several kinds of output. For the user the most
important are final reports, but there should also be options for providing detailed intermediate results from various segments of the simulation and a complete file of data which can be used for restarting. For
time-dependent simulations, the restart capability is particularly useful.

In addition to user data, a well-designed simulator will have internal debugging or tracing output for aiding the programmer support
group. Large software packages, such as simulation programs, are
frequently modified to correct inadequacies, make enhancements, or to
rectify downright errors. Even mature software will produce spurious
results for some unusual combinations of data.

Simulation packages can be highly effective training tools. If
training is a primary use, care should be taken to provide realistic
input and output so that the trainee can gain the most insight from
the experience.

Various forms of output, numerical tables, textual reports, and
plots are possible. A mix of these modes can be very effective in presenting results.

The simulation of the hydraulic network provided the following
output.

Pipe number	Flow rate	Pressure drop (psi)
1	414.03	0.652
2	385.97	1.154
3	85.97	0.028
4	122.27	0.543
5	291.76	0.048
6	291.76	0.482
7	24.99	0.017
8	108.24	0.007
9	83.25	0.024
10	16.75	0.007
11	91.76	0.049

A full report from the simulation would include a list of the input data and the sum of pressure drops around each loop.

7.7 ANALYSIS PHASE

Analysis is one of the iterative activities which ends only because a limit is set to the time or resources spent on it. After each set of simulation runs, results are obtained and should be analyzed. The two prototype modes of analysis can be employed: question the results, and compare them to both other reported information and expected results.

During the questioning mode, the simulation output is scanned for reasonableness. Any anomalous results should be noted and an effort made to determine the cause of the anomaly. This is also the time to determine if the original objectives have been met and all of the originally posed questions answered. If inconclusive results are obtained, recommended actions are required to settle the issue or restate the issue based upon the insight gained. This might take the form of several new insightful questions which need answers.

During the comparison mode of analysis, the history-matching effort can be discussed. It should be noted where average properties were used, which aspects of the simulation are most likely to deviate from the average, in which direction they will deviate, and why. If the system is subject to uncontrollable outside influences, these should be discussed. Any methods for compensating for the external effects should be described in detail.

It is possible during this mode to uncover points of conflict between either two or more results of the simulation or between the simulation output and other reported results. Resolving such conflicts is usually one of the more fruitful avenues for gaining insight into the system.

There are several potential sources of discrepancies in simulation results which can be scrutinized during the analysis phase:

1. The model itself is usually approximate, involving assumptions, using averages, and containing omissions.

2. If the mathematical model contains differential equations or integral equations, these will have been replaced by discrete approximations such as finite difference representation or numerical quadrature.

3. The exact solution of the discrete representation is not obtained due to the round-off error incurred from using a computer with finite word length.

4. The input data are inaccurate, averages, or poorly known assumptions.

Errors from any one or all four sources can be significant. Some effort can be made to estimate or control errors due to discrete representation of continuous equations or finite word length. These estimates are usually the responsibility of the model developer or program analyst. Errors due to poor data are difficult to assess but are the responsibility of the user.

In many instances, the engineer is less concerned with the absolute accuracy than with the effects of changing variables. Such sensitivity can be determined by making a planned series of runs. The trends from these runs can then provide the information sought.

One useful approach in analyzing results is to list all of the attributes of the system, such as its physical dimensions, color, shape, mass, velocity, cost, function, etc. Once the attributes have been listed, they can be categorized, compared, checked for completeness, and used to relate to the objectives. Any patterns which emerge can be useful in forming new or original conceptual units which can lead to further insight.

A positive outcome of any analysis phase is to restate the objectives more clearly and in terms which are measurable. The abstract objective must be translated into an action statement with a measurable result. Relative terms such as "adequate" have to be defined more specifically. A measurable objective is one for which attainment is clearly defined.

The larger the scale of the simulation, the more detailed data are required, and the more expertise (frequently from disparate fields) is required. Having experts from several disciplines working together necessitates a degree of coordination, but it also can lead, through cooperation, to synergistic effects in which the result is greater than the sum of the individual contributions. The analysis phase is the area in which most of these benefits will result.

7.8 USING PERSONAL COMPUTERS

There are two major factors affecting the use of any particular computer for simulation: size and speed. As usual in computing, there are some trade-offs between these two factors. The size of the problem that can be handled can usually be increased by decomposing the problem and swapping information between core storage and some larger peripheral memory device such as a disk. This swapping consumes time that could normally be spent in calculation if the entire problem could reside permanently in core.

Some manufacturers of mainframe computers have developed the concept of virtual storage to relieve programmers from concerns about secondary storage. In effect, computers with virtual storage let the operating system do the swapping between core storage and peripheral devices as needed. This is done in a manner which is transparent to the programmer and the user. Until the operating systems of personal computers evolve into virtual storage systems, developers of simulation systems for the personal computers will have to concern themselves with the trade-offs between size and speed.

Barring the availability of a virtual memory operating system, there are basically only two approaches to take for handling a simulation too large to fit in the computer at one time: decomposition and simplification. Decomposition retains the details of mathematical description but can require significant effort to break the simulation into segments without sacrificing speed. Simplification frequently speeds up computation, but at the cost of losing details of computation and frequently with the unacceptable effect of distorting the phenomenological representation. Some preliminary efforts have been made using both of these techniques specifically for personal computers [4].

7.8.1 Decomposition

There are two system capabilities, one software and one hardware, required to allow effective decomposition. These are: (1) some form of chaining or overlaying, and (2) efficient peripheral storage.

Chaining or Overlaying

Chaining or overlaying is an operating software feature which allows successive pieces of code to be read from peripheral storage into the central processor for execution. Each segment of code uses some of the same locations in core so they are said to be "overlayed." The values for variables needed to communicate between the successive segments are stored in an area of core which is not overlayed and are therefore available at all times. The simulation software developer is responsible for dividing the code into segments which will fit in the overlay portion of core in such a way that computation speed is maximized, a task that is neither easy nor straightforward.

Peripheral Storage

Efficient peripheral storage is currently available in the form of hard disks. Floppy disks might not store sufficient data to contain a simulation on one diskette and would be prohibitively slow if any switching of diskettes were involved. Even without switching diskettes, reading and writing floppies is one or two orders of magnitude slower than input/output (I/O) on a hard disk, aggravating the problem with computational speed reduction due to chaining or overlaying. Improvements in other storage media, such as bubble or bulk memory, will eventually lead to peripheral storage devices without the relative slowness and mechanical fragility of rotating disks. Magnetic tapes, because of their sequential I/O nature, are inherently impractical as storage media for chaining or overlaying processes.

Simulations can be broken into three major phases: (1) data input, (2) iterative computation, and (3) reporting or output. These major phases logically follow each other in sequence and provide natural and effective points for decomposition of the software.

The input and output phases usually occur only once each and can be readily decomposed into manageable segments without significant increases in computer time. The iterative computation phase is where most of the computer time is accrued, and, although by its nature it is the most difficult to decompose effectively, it will most likely require decomposition into subphases.

7.8.2 Simplification

It is necessary to discuss both converting existing software and developing software from scratch. Programs written for larger computers frequently have bell and whistle enhancements which have been added to increase convenience or beautify output and sometimes extensive sections of code to handle special cases. Such enhancements can be eliminated when modifying the software for use on a personal computer.

Further reduction in program size can be attained by replacing general purpose procedures by specific purpose procedures. For example: if the existing software contains a general root-finding procedure, this might be replaced by a simpler root-finding method specific to the equation(s) in the problem of immediate concern.

The idea is to eliminate frills and replace complex procedures with simpler procedures. Versatility, such as allowing input to be in any of several different systems of units, can also be pared down with a consequent reduction in program size but without sacrificing the accuracy of the representation.

When converting an existing program there is a fat body of software which is being pared down, but, when developing a simulation from scratch, the winnowing of potential methods is done at the conceptual level—before any code is written—and then iteratively as validation procedures are applied. All of the characteristics of good software discussed in Section 6.4 can be built-in.

7.9 USE OF GRAPHICS

Only a few scattered simulation programs developed for mainframe computers include any appreciable graphics. This is not so much from lack of foresight as from lack of technology availability at the time of the development. In contrast, the personal computer grew out of a generation of computers in which graphics and animation were the prime reasons for their existence. The result is that models and simulations being developed by individuals with personal computer backgrounds are presenting information in forms unheard of (except in the specialized area of computer-aided drafting) as recently as a few years ago.

Output in the form of line, bar, pie, and surface charts have been produced for many years, through the use of plotters and printers. But, with the widespread use of cathods ray tubes (CRTs or video displays), and in particular color CRTs, as the primary output device, not only are static graphs such as those forms mentioned above possible, but animations are too. This opens up an entirely new realm of information presentation which has yet to be signiftcantly exploited for other than arcade-type games. The boss doesn't want to play animated star wars, but he might want to play animated price wars. The dynamics of market forces; the research and development cycle; local demographics as a function of time; all kinds of factors affecting business and engineering decisions can be depicted in vivid color to assist in decisionmaking and creative processes.

The old Chinese saying "a picture is worth a thousand words" certainly applies to computer output. But not every simulation requires graphical displays. The table below can be used as a screening guide for identifying those characteristics which would indicate that graphics output was highly desirable.

Screening Guide for Graphics

Situation changes with time

    Dynamic respose must be measured
    Operator response time is critical
    Process is operating near constraints
    Disorientation of operator is possible
    Spatial relationships between objects change

High density of information

    Operator is at a distance from display
    Complex configuration of process
    Complex functional relationship between variables
    Statistical inference required—scattered data

The simple hydraulic network simulation now has been run and meets the basic objectives. However, there are a myriad of other improvements which could be made to the program to enhance its utility. To name a few, in the area of making the user interface more convenient, there are several enhancements that come to mind:

1. Graphically display the network with flows, pressures, and other system parameters as desired.

2. Have an archival option to save and retrieve:
    (a) Network description
    (b) Flow rates, pressures, etc.
    (c) Descriptive information

3. Have the program make the initial flow distribution from the external flows.

In addition to making the user interface more convenient, some possible enhancements to increase the versatility of the program would include:

1. Allow branches that are not in any loop.

2. Allow input and output in various units.

3. Add the capability to handle pumps.

The computational efficiency could be improved by the following:

1. Use a simpler routine for calculating the friction factor and the associated correction factor, R.

2. Identify those parts of the friction factor equation that are used in determining R and pass the values between the f and R routines to save duplicate computations.

If the same problem arose for fluids other than water, the software could be expanded to calculate properties such as viscosity and density from composition and operating conditions.

The enhancements mentioned above could, by and large, be implemented individually, as desired. Such incremental enhancement allows improvements in a prioritized, staged basis and is relatively easy to manage. It is common practice for the developers to have three versions of a given simulation system: (1) the production system for general use, (2) an on-trial version that is being tried out by the adventurous users and at the same time is being debugged, and (3) a developmental version for experimentation by the software developers. The natural progression is from experimental to on-trial to production versions.

Valid applications of large-scale simulations generally possess the following three features: (1) a properly formulated, measurable objective of economic significance, (2) sufficiently accurate critical data describing the system under study, and (3) the answers to the questions posed are not obvious, usually because there are too many interacting elements involved.

Applications of sophisticated simulation packages to insignificant problems is a waste of resources. It is also inappropriate to use such programs when the critical input data are poorly known. "Garbage in-- Garbage out" still rules.

REFERENCES

1. Bressand, A., "Mastering the World Economy," *Foreign Affairs*, Spring 1983, pp. 745--772.
2. ASPEN, Advanced System for Process Engineering, Aspen Tech, Cambridge, Massachussetts (1979).
3. Ingels, D., PRODYC, A System for Process Dynamics and Control, Ph.D. dissertation, University of Houston, 1970.
4. Soesianto, F., and R. E J. Soesiarto, "Microcomputer Simulation of Petroleum Reservoirs," *Proceed. Indonesian Petr. Assoc.*, 13th Ann. Convention, Jakarta, Indonesia, May 1984, pp. 261--269.

APPENDIX

The following program simulates Hardy Cross equilibrium, and Churchill's friction factor, f.

```
1000  REM  MODIFIED HARDY CROSS
1005 FI = 3.1415928:GC = 32.14:K3 = 3600
1010  DIM FL(50),D(50),L(50),RU(50),CF(50),NO(50),NT(50),M(50),LP(20,50)
1015  GOSUB 1800: REM    GET INPUT DATA > > > > >
1020  FOR I = 1 TO TF: REM    CONVERT DIAMS TO FT, FL TO PER SEC
1025 D(I) = D(I) / 12
1030 M(I) = FL(I) / K3
1035  NEXT I
1040 VF = VF * .672E - 3: REM  VISCOSITY TO LB/(FT-SEC)
1045  FOR IT = 1 TO MI: REM       = = = = = = = =
1047 SO = 0
1050  FOR IL = 1 TO TL: REM    LOOP LOOP + + + + +
1055 SP = 0:SR = 0
1060 XP = PL(IL)
1070  FOR J = 1 TO XP: REM    PIPES/LOOP - - - -
1075 NN = LP(IL,J)
1077 ET = RU(NN):DI = D(NN):LE = L(NN)
1080  IF (M(NN) < > 0) THEN  GOTO 1090
1085 DP(NN) = 0:R = 1: GOTO 1135
1090  IF (CF(NN) = 0) THEN  GOTO 1100: REM    IS IT COMMON
1095 M(NN) =  - M(NN)
1100 MF =  ABS (M(NN))
1105 RE = 4 * MF / (FI * D(NN) * VF)
1125  GOSUB 3000: REM  GET FRIC FAC  > > > > >
1130 DP(NN) = 8 * F * LE * MF * M(NN) / (FI * FI * GC * DF * DI ^ 5)
1135 SP = SP + DP(NN)
1140  GOSUB 4000: REM  GET R  > > > > > > > >
1142  PRINT "IT,NN,R ";IT,NN,R
1145 SR = SR + R
1146  IF (KT = 0) THEN  GOTO 1150
1147  PRINT "IL,J,NN ";IL; SPC( 2);J; SPC( 3);NN
```

```
1150  NEXT J: REM      - - - - - - - - - - -
1155  DQ =  - SF / SR:SQ = SQ +  ABS (DQ)
1160  FOR J = 1 TO XP: REM    * * * * * * * *
1165  NN = LP(IL,J)
1170  M(NN) = M(NN) + DQ
1172  IF (KT = 0) THEN  GOTO 1175
1173  PRINT " IL=";IL; SPC( 2);" DQ=";DQ; SPC( 2);" NN=";NN; SPC( 2);" NEW
      M=";M(NN)
1174  INPUT "HIT RETURN TO CONTINUE ";A$
1175  NEXT J: REM      * * * * * * * * * * *
1180  NEXT IL: REM     + + + + + + + + + + +
1190  REM    C H E C K   F O R   C O N V E R G E N C E
1192  IF (KT = 0) THEN  GOTO 1195
1193  INVERSE : PRINT " ITER# ";IT;" SUM Q= ";SQ: NORMAL
1195  IF (SQ < CT) THEN  GOTO 1205
1200  NEXT IT: REM     = = = = = = = = = = =
1205  GOSUB 1900: REM     CALL OUTPUT ROUTINE    > > > >
1210  INPUT " ENTER C TO CONTINUE, OTHER CHAR TO STOP ";A$
1215  IF (A$ = "C") THEN  GOTO 1015
1220  END
```

Subroutine 1

```
1800  HOME : REM    INPUT DATA FOR H.C. < < < ---
1805  INVERSE : PRINT "M O D I F I E D   H A R D Y   C R O S S ": PRINT "
      ": PRINT " "
1810  INPUT "  ENTER TITLE, 1 LINE OR LESS ";TI$: PRINT " ": PRINT "C O N
      F I G U R A T I O N   D A T A"
1815  INPUT "  ENTER TOTAL # PIPES IN NETWORK ";TP
1817  INPUT "  ENTER TOTAL # LOOPS IN NETWORK ";TL
1819  INPUT "  ENTER TOTAL # NODES IN NETWORK ";TN: PRINT " ": PRINT "F L
      U I D   P R O P E R T I E S": PRINT " "
1821  INPUT "  ENTER FLUID VISCOSITY, CP ";VF
1823  INPUT "  ENTER FLUID DENSITY, LM/CUBIC FT ";DF: PRINT " ": PRINT "L
      O O P   D A T A": PRINT " "
1825  INPUT "  ENTER CONVERGENCE TOLERENCE ";CT
1827  INPUT "  ENTER MAX ITER & TRACE FLAG ";MI,KT
1829  PRINT "  ENTER NUMBER OF PIPES PER LOOP ": FOR J = 1 TO TL
1831  PRINT " FOR LOOP ";J: INPUT PL(J)
1833  NEXT J
1835  FOR I = 1 TO TL: REM  GET PIPE NOS. IN EACH LOOP
1837  PRINT " FOR LOOP # ";I;" ENTER PIPE NUMBERS"
1839  NP = PL(I): FOR J = 1 TO NP
1841  PRINT " ENTER PIPE # FOR POSITION ";J: INPUT LP(I,J)
1843  NEXT J
1845  NEXT I
1847  HOME : PRINT " ": PRINT "P I P E   D A T A": PRINT " "
1849  FOR J = 1 TO TP
1851  PRINT "  ENTER NODES ORIGIN TERMIN COMMON LEN DIA RUF"
1853  PRINT " FOR PIPE # ";J
1855  INPUT NO(J),NT(J),CP(J),L(J),D(J),RU(J)
1857  NEXT J
1858  NORMAL
1860  PRINT " ": INVERSE : PRINT " ENTER INITIAL FLOWS, LB/HR "
1865  FOR J = 1 TO TP
1870  PRINT " PIPE # ";J: INPUT FL(J)
1875  NEXT J
1880  NORMAL : RETURN : END
```

Subroutine 2

```
1900  REM  OUTPUT FOR HARDY CROSS
1902  PRINT " TOTAL ITERATIONS = ";IT: INPUT "ENTER C TO CONTINUE";A$
1905  PRINT "  PIPE NO.    FLOW    DELTA P"
1910  FOR I = 1 TO TP
1920  DH = DP(I) / 144: REM  CONVERT LB/SQFT TO LB/SQIN
1930  FO = M(I) * K3: REM     "   LB/SEC TO LB/HR
1940  PRINT I,FO,DH
1950  NEXT I
1960  RETURN
1970  END
```

Subroutine 3

```
3000  REM  CHURCHILL'S FRICTION FACTOR, CHE 7NOV77
3005  REM  INPUT ET,  DI,  RE
3010  REM  OUTPUT F
3015  C1 = .08333333: IF (RE > = 2100) THEN  GOTO 3025
3020  F = 64 / RE: GOTO 3070
3025  A = (2.457 *  LOG (1 / ((7 / RE) ^ .9 + .27 * ET / DI))) ^ 16
3030  B = (37530 / RE) ^ 16
3035  F1 = 8 / RE
3040  REM  CHECK FOR POSSIBLE UNDERFLOW < < < -
3045  IF (F1 > = 1.E - 6) THEN  GOTO 3060
3050  F2 = 0
3055  GOTO 3065
3060  F2 = F1 ^ 12
3065  F = 8 * (F2 + 1 / (A + B) ^ 1.5) ^ C1
3070  RETURN : END
```

Subroutine 4

```
4000  REM  CHURCHILLS R
4010  REM  CORRECTION FACTOR, R FOR CHURCHILL'S FRIC FAC
4013  DD = DI * DI
4015  PI = 3.1415928:B1 = 2.457:GC = 32.14
4017  RE = 4 * MF / (PI * DI * VF)
4018  IF (RE < 2100) THEN  GOTO 4140
4020  C2 = PI * VF * DI
4025  A1 = 2 * C2
4030  C1 = 7 * C2 / 4
4035  D1 = .27 * ET / DI
4040  E1 = 9382.5 * C2
4045  E9 = MF ^ .9
4050  C9 = C1 ^ .9
4055  C3 = C9 + E9 * D1
4060  DE = E9 / C3: REM                    DELTA
4065  D3 = .9 / (MF ^ .1 * C3) - .9 * MF ^ .8 * D1 / (C3 * C3): REM  EQ. 30
```

```
4070 DS = B1 * D3 / DE: REM                                    EQ.  29
4075 PS = B1 *  LOG (DE): REM                                  EQ.  26
4080 E2 = (E1 / MF) ^ 16: REM
4085 DH = 16 * (PS ^ 15 * DS - E2 / MF): REM                          EQ.  27
4090 FH = PS ^ 16 + E2:PX = FH ^ 1.5: REM      EQ  22
4095 A0 = (A1 / MF) ^ 12
4100 DU =  - 12 * A0 / MF - (1.5 * DH / FH) / PX: REM        EQ 23B
4105 U = A0 + 1 / PX: REM      EQ   20
4110 X1 =  - 11 / 12
4115 FD = (2 / 3) * U ^ X1 * DU: REM  DF/DM                    EQ. 21
4130 R =  ABS (DP(NN)) * (2 / MF + FD / F): REM    EQ   38
4132  IF (KT = 0) THEN  GOTO 4135
4133  PRINT " R, MF, DF/DM ";R,MF,FD
4135  RETURN
4140 R = 2048 * LE * VF / (DF * PI * PI * PI * DD * DD * DD): REM        EQ.
       13
4145  GOTO 4135: END
```

INDEX